Our Lady, Undoer of Knots
A Living Novena

"Exceptional and inspiring, this armchair pilgrimage and prayer guide will help to untangle even the most vicious knots in our lives. Combining Pope Francis's Holy Land pilgrimage, her own pilgrimage experiences, and the seventeenth-century novena to *Our Lady, Undoer of Knots*, Marge Fenelon fashioned this heartfelt novena. A must read!"

Donna-Marie Cooper O'Boyle
EWTN host and author of *Rooted in Love*

"Marge Fenelon shares her Holy Land pilgrimage with reflections on the knots that impede peace there, creatively comparing them to the knots in our soul that impede our interior peace. The novena invites us to join Pope Francis in presenting the knots of our soul to the Father of mercy through Mary, the Undoer of Knots."

Most Rev. Kevin C. Rhoades
Bishop of Fort Wayne-South Bend Diocese

"As I read this book, many times did I feel that the Holy Spirit was speaking to my heart as I recalled my own trip to the Holy Land. Using the form of a novena, Marge Fenelon takes us on a journey through the sacred sites visited by the Holy Father during his historic pilgrimage. Each day tackles a different knot—injustice, separation, confusion, hopelessness, grief and loss, discord, betrayal, envy and pride, and affliction—both as they relate to the situation in the land where Jesus lived as well as in our own lives. It was a joy reading this book."

Diana von Glahn
Producer and host of *The Faithful Traveler*

"In *Our Lady, Undoer of Knots,* Marge Fenelon has written the book I wish I had written! Marge's beautiful, evocative and poetic application of the devotion to a pilgrimage in the Holy Land takes my breath away. I not only feel like I have walked the ground where Jesus and Mary walked, but Marge's heartfelt prayers and meditations opened a deeper appreciation of the way Mary does undo the knots of our lives—if we invite her in. Whether you read it as an armchair pilgrimage or as a devotional or use it to pray a novena, this guided meditation is an absolute treasure of faith."

Woodeene Koenig-Bricker
Author of *365 Saints*

"Pope Francis brought *Our Lady, Undoer of Knots* out of obscurity into a living reality for our everyday lives. Marge Fenelon has taken this reality and provided a roadmap enveloped in a novena tied to the Holy Land to help us untie the most common knots that prevent us from living a truly joy-filled life. This book will help you firmly place the ribbon of your life in the hands of Our Lady where she will become your advocate in ways you never imagined possible. Buy this book. Read it, pray with it and then share it with someone you know who is searching for freedom from a troubled heart."

Lisa Wheeler
Founder of Carmel Communications

A Guided Meditation from the Holy Land

Marge Fenelon

Founded in 1865, Ave Maria Press is a ministry of the United States Province of Holy Cross.

www.avemariapress.com

Paperback: ISBN-13 978-1-59471-630-0

E-book: ISBN-13 978-1-59471-631-7

Cover and text design by Katherine Coleman.

Printed and bound in the United States of America.

Library of Congress Cataloging-in-Publication Data

First and foremost,

this is dedicated to the Fenelon Clan.

Then, to Fr. Joseph Kentenich (1885–1968),

whose words and example

have influenced my entire life.

Contents

Foreword

Knots. Bumps in the road. Thorns in the side. Rough edges. Call them what you will, but we all have them: those difficulties in life that make life knotty, bumpy, thorny, or rough. Some of them are, unfortunately, of our own creation—we make bad choices and things get complicated. Others come of the craziness that is life—illness, misunderstandings, unforeseen situations. While I certainly couldn't begin to explain the reasons or solutions for the many knots in life, I can say with 100 percent certainty that we *all* have them.

But our good God never leaves us without divine assistance. In response to the original knot of sin tied by Eve in the Garden long ago, he has lovingly given us the great Undoer of Knots, his Mother, the Blessed Virgin Mary.

I remember the first time I heard about the devotion to Mary under the title "Our Lady, Undoer (or 'Untier') of Knots," the devotion dear to Pope Francis's heart. I was preparing for a very exciting trip to the Holy Land in May of 2014 to film a special program about the pope's pilgrimage to the Holy Land for my television series, *The Faithful Traveler.* There was so much to do in preparation for this exciting trip, and I had a lot on my mind. I was blessed to have traveled to the Holy Land once before in 2011, when Select International Tours had invited us to film the Archdiocese of Philadelphia's pilgrimage to the Holy Land, resulting in our series, *The Faithful Traveler in the Holy Land*. It was an amazing and unexpected blessing to have been able to visit such an amazing place; I was grateful for having gone. I never expected to go again.

Shortly after *The Faithful Traveler in the Holy Land* broadcast on EWTN, we were contacted by the Israel Ministry of Tourism with an invitation to return to the Holy Land for Pope Francis's historic pilgrimage. The Jordan Tourism Board graciously agreed to sponsor our Jordanian leg of the trip, and friends in Bethlehem agreed to help us on the third leg. We were all set. Three of our friends agreed to help us document the historic trip and with a team of five—three more than we normally have—our plans were both lofty and enthusiastic.

On May 11, 2014, nine days before our departure, my husband, who is also coproducer, director, and cameraman for *The Faithful Traveler*, had a heart attack, leaving him unable to make the trip. The thought of leaving him to fly to the Holy Land to film a television series seemed ludicrous, but I felt an obligation to the tourism offices that had been so generous to us, plus the historic significance of the event was so enormous, and my mother was already flying out from California to watch our dog. Now, she'd be minding David, too. Shortly after this event, another of our cameramen fell ill with the flu, knocking our crew down from five to four to three.

My mind reeled. The knots were many. Still, we went.

The trip was difficult. My production plans had to be completely reworked multiple times, before and during the shoot. The stress of my husband's illness and absence rendered me overly emotional, casting a pall over our production. We lost some expensive equipment.

A month after our trip, fighting broke out between Israel and Palestine and things haven't been the same ever since.

It's easy to look at these knots and think they are tangled beyond hope. But as a woman of faith, I know that in God, all things are possible, including peace in the Holy Land.

So I pray. The Holy Father has asked us to pray unceasingly for peace in the Holy Land, and this little book is the perfect tool for that task. Using the form of a novena—that nine-day prayer modeled after the nine days the Blessed Mother and Jesus' disciples spent praying between Jesus' Ascension into Heaven and the Descent of the Holy Spirit at Pentecost—Marge Fenelon takes us on a journey through the sacred sites visited by the Holy Father during his historic pilgrimage. Each day tackles a different knot—injustice, separation, confusion, hopelessness, grief and loss, discord, betrayal, envy and pride, and affliction—both as they relate to the situation in the land where Jesus lived as well as in our own lives.

What will come of praying this living novena? What is in my future? What is in your future? What is in the future of the Holy Land? No one but God has these answers. As Christians, we are not called to know or even want to know the future; we are called to turn to Our Lord and His Mother with confidence, and entrust to them the ribbons of our lives.

Let us use this marvelous book to do just that.

Diana von Glahn
Producer and Host of *The Faithful Traveler*

Acknowledgments

I owe volumes of gratitude to a number of people who contributed in one way or another to this manuscript.

First, of course, is the Fenelon Clan, who were my greatest cheerleaders in every step of my trip to Israel with the Catholic Press Association—from applying all the way through decompressing once I'd returned home.

I'm grateful to the Catholic Press Association for providing the opportunity, and the Israel Ministry of Tourism for hosting it. I'd especially like to thank our IMOT escort, Jill Daly, and guide, Ron Harai, for coordinating, informing, and sustaining us throughout the trip.

My fellow travelers from the Catholic Press Association—Denise Bossert, John Fiester, Julie Holthaus, and Peter Jesserer Smith—ever so patiently put up with my quirks. I'm especially grateful to them for their graciousness and safeguarding at Masada.

Diana von Glahn has rooted for me from conception to birth of this book. I'm humbled and grateful that she's agreed to write the foreword.

Finally, I absolutely owe a mountain of gratitude to my editor, Heidi Saxton, one of the best editors I've ever worked with, who saw me through all the struggles, spiritual warfare, uncertainty, and blunders that I faced as I worked on this manuscript. She was also there to rejoice with me over the successes. We are both most grateful to Our Lady, Undoer of Knots, whose loving presence was with us every step of the way.

Introduction

During his October 12, 2013, catechesis, Pope Francis revealed to the world his special devotion to the Blessed Virgin Mary under the title Our Lady, Undoer of Knots. In his address, he spoke of Mary as the "new Eve" who unties the knot of Eve's disobedience. He also mentioned that Mary undoes other kinds of knots as well. "When we do not listen to [God], when we do not follow his will, we do concrete things that demonstrate our lack of trust in him—for that is what sin is—and a kind of knot is created deep within us. These knots take away our peace and serenity. They are dangerous, since many knots can form a tangle which gets more and more painful and difficult to undo," he said.[1]

The Holy Father encountered the image of Our Lady, Undoer of Knots, while he was stationed in Germany in 1986 studying for his doctorate. He visited the church of St. Peter am Perlach and saw the painting of Our Lady, Undoer of Knots. In the painting, Mary holds a knotted ribbon in her hands—representing our lives and the knots that cause us suffering—and patiently works to untie the knots. He was captivated by both the painting and the story behind it. He bought a postcard of the image and took it back with him to Argentina. As a cardinal, he had the image engraved into a chalice and presented it to Pope Benedict XVI. Later in his life, Our Lady, Undoer of Knots, saw him through a very difficult time, deepening his devotion to, and appreciation of, Our Lady under that title. Because of this, author Paul Vallely titled his biography of Pope Francis *Untying the Knots*.

It's no surprise, then, that as a result of Pope Francis's enthusiasm for Our Lady, Undoer of Knots, the devotion spread throughout Argentina and continues to spread throughout the world. It is also not surprising that the first thing Pope Francis did after his election was to visit the Basilica of Santa Maria Maggiore and place his papacy under Mary's care. As before his election, he continues to promote devotion to Our Lady, Undoer of Knots, as pope.

If Our Lady, Undoer of Knots, unties the knots of disobedience to God's will, then we can imagine that Pope Francis turned to her in his plea for peace in the Holy Land. God doesn't will us to be in constant conflict; he wills us to live in peace and freedom. That was the pope's message when he visited the Holy Land May 24–26, 2014. Since then, he's asked us again and again to join him in praying for peace in this war-torn region.

In May 2014, I traveled to the Holy Land with the Catholic Press Association as part of Pope Francis's pilgrimage. We spent ten days in Israel, visiting the holy sites and getting to know the country. I approached the trip with a professional attitude—I was there on business. I soon discovered that it was impossible (at least for me) to be in the Holy Land without being deeply touched by the land's history and significance and interiorly changed by the experience. It was amazing to be there, covering the excitement of the pope's visit, but I could see that God had led me there for another purpose—to take in the Holy Land's richness and allow it to enrich my perspective of the Catholic faith.

Pope Francis's primary message and petition in the Holy Land was for an end to the conflict and the initiation of a lasting peace. I contemplated this time and again while I was there, and made it a point to pray often for peace. In my contemplation, however, I realized that peace begins on the inside, not the outside. Peace, wherever in the world, begins in our communities, our parishes, our homes, and in our hearts. Conflict doesn't only occur in the Middle East; it occurs in our personal lives as well, and even at our dinner tables. I began to pray for that kind of peace.

During my prayer and reflection, I was reminded of Pope Francis's devotion to Our Lady, Undoer of Knots, and my own introduction to it some years back. I'd heard a homily by a very holy and well-educated priest in which he mentioned Our Lady, Undoer of Knots, and the power of her intercession. Curious, I had researched the devotion's origin (more on that on pages 121–124) and felt an immediate impulse to pray the novena for the knots I had in my own life. It worked, and I've since prayed the novena in other circumstances and seen many small miracles as a result.

I'd like to see the same for you, so I'm sharing with you this novena to Our Lady, Undoer of Knots, organized around Pope Francis's Holy Land pilgrimage and his urgent request that we pray for peace there. As we place into her hands the task of untying the knots of contention, violence, and unrest in the Middle East, we can also open ourselves to Our Lady and her ability to untie the knots of our own lives: our fears and conflicts, and all that robs us of our own peace. As we make our way through the novena, and place ourselves in the homeland of the Holy Family, we can trust God to send us the miracles we need most.

How to Pray A Living Novena

A novena is a form of Catholic devotion that involves offering special prayers or services for nine consecutive days (*novena* means "nine") for a particular intention. This practice can be traced back to apostolic times, when the apostles and Mary gathered in the Upper Room for nine days after the Lord ascended to heaven (see Acts 1–2). On the tenth day, the Holy Spirit descended upon them at Pentecost. Over time, particular novenas dedicated to particular saints or for particular seasons or intentions began to spring up in every time and place.

This book offers a unique kind of prayer experience, a "living novena" or a kind of extended guided meditation. By reading one chapter of the book each day, you will be able to experience a kind of "armchair pilgrimage," following the journeys of Pope Francis and myself and listening to the Holy Father's words as a starting point for your own reflection.

Each day, as we examine one of these holy places, the physical landscape of the Holy Land and the historical and scriptural accounts of the life of Jesus and Mary will guide you to think about the "knots" of your interior landscape.

Then, we'll petition Our Lady, Undoer of Knots, together to undo the knots in our lives—injustice, separation, confusion, hopelessness, grief and sorrow, discord, betrayal, envy and pride, and affliction. By releasing these knots into her hands, we'll begin working toward the peace for which we all long, in our own lives and in the world.

At the end of each chapter are questions for meditation. I hope you take them seriously, bringing them into your prayer time and opening yourself to the work of the Holy Spirit in your heart and soul. It can be intimidating to be frank with ourselves, and to truthfully admit what's going on inside of us. But, unless we do that, we'll never move toward peace.

I encourage you to meditate often on the image of Our Lady, Undoer of Knots. When you look at it, you'll see the ribbon in her hands that represents your life—the life God wants you to live in freedom, holiness, and peace. The ribbon is knotted, and each knot stops you from proceeding on your journey to fulfill God's will and grow in his grace and mercy. You might want to try making the image your own by acknowledging the knots in your life and matching them to a specific knot in the picture. Allow yourself to come so close to Our Lady that you could imagine yourself sitting at her feet, watching her untie your knots.

As we embark on this journey with Pope Francis and Our Lady, Undoer of Knots, let's allow the Holy Father's words to encourage us: "Do I ask Mary to help me trust in God's mercy, to undo those knots, to change? She, as a woman of faith, will surely tell you: 'Get up, go to the Lord: he understands you.' And she leads us by the hand as a Mother, our Mother, to the embrace of our Father, the Father of mercies."[2]

I wish you every blessing, and pray that the knots in the ribbon of your life be undone, through the intercession of Our Lady, Undoer of Knots!

Day One: Bethany Beyond the Jordan

The Knot of Injustice

You young people, my dear young friends, you have a particular sensitivity towards injustice, but you are often disappointed by facts that speak of corruption on the part of people who put their own interests before the common good. To you and to all, I repeat: never yield to discouragement, do not lose trust, do not allow your hope to be extinguished. Situations can change, people can change. Be the first to seek to bring good, do not grow accustomed to evil, but defeat it with good. The Church is

> with you, bringing you the precious good of faith, bringing Jesus Christ, who "came that they may have life and have it abundantly" (Jn 10:10).
>
> —Pope Francis[1]

To witness injustice, all you have to do is open a newspaper or click on a media website. Religious persecution, abortion, cultural discrimination, murder, theft, and more can be seen on every page. Wherever there is violation of rights or inequality, there is injustice. Injustice often provokes anger, and anger born of injustice can lead to conflict.

Sadly, injustice isn't only found in the news; it can be found in our personal lives as well. Any time we're treated unfairly, it can be a type of injustice. We see minor injustices on a daily basis, like when another driver refuses to let us into the highway lane, or when someone cuts in front of us in the grocery line. We might also see bigger injustices, like receiving an unfair court settlement or being blamed for someone else's mistake at work. Injustice is hard to bear in any form.

Signs from the Holy Land: Crossing the Jordan

The pope's first stop in the Holy Land was Amman, Jordan. There, he greeted the king and queen of Jordan, met with the authorities of the kingdom, celebrated Mass in Amman's International Stadium, and met with refugees and disabled young people in the Latin Church at Bethany Beyond the Jordan. It was a full day, to say the least.

But the Holy Father also visited the place believed to be the baptismal site of Jesus on the Jordan River. The area has been known since earliest times, and in modern history it was made into a national park of the Kingdom of Jordan called Bethany Beyond the Jordan. His stop there was brief, but his joy and devotion will leave a lasting effect on my heart.

I've many times pondered the text of Pope Francis's homily during Mass in the International Stadium. There's just so much "meat" to it. He explained that the Holy Spirit descended upon Jesus so as to prepare him for his mission of salvation—the mission of a humble, meek servant. He also explained that, just as the Holy Spirit anointed Jesus for his mission, he also anoints us for our God-given mission.

> The Holy Spirit . . . anointed Jesus inwardly and he anoints his disciples, so that they can have the mind of Christ and thus be disposed to live lives of peace and communion. Through the anointing of the Spirit, our human nature is sealed with the holiness of Jesus Christ and we are enabled to love our brothers and sisters with the same love which God has for us. We ought, therefore, to show concrete signs of humility, fraternity,

> forgiveness and reconciliation. These signs are the prerequisite of a true, stable, and lasting peace. Let us ask the Father to anoint us so that we may fully become his children, ever more conformed to Christ, and may learn to see one another as brothers and sisters. Thus, by putting aside our grievances and divisions, we can show fraternal love for one another. This is what Jesus asks of us in the Gospel: "If you love me, you will keep my commandments. And I will pray the Father, and he will give you another Advocate, to be with you always" (Jn 14:15–16).[2]

Our missions aren't always clear to us, and we tend to forget that we're anointed for a special purpose on this earth. When we're suffering an injustice, we can feel spurned rather than anointed. Is it possible that Jesus felt this way at times, as well?

Just after his baptism, Jesus went into the dessert to pray for forty days and nights in order to ready himself for what lay ahead. We, too, are anointed by the same Spirit who anointed Jesus himself, in order to be sent out, in the words of Pope Francis, "as messengers and witnesses of peace."

The Spirit sends us out to be messengers and witnesses of peace, despite the injustices going on around us. That's a tall order, but with the Spirit's help, we can do it. Listen to these concluding thoughts from Pope Francis:

> Dear friends! Dear brothers and sisters! The Holy Spirit descended upon Jesus in the Jordan and thus inaugurated his work of redemption to free the world from sin and death. Let us ask the Spirit to prepare our hearts to encounter our brothers and sisters, so that we may overcome our differences rooted in political thinking, language, culture, and religion. Let us ask him to anoint our whole being with the oil of his mercy, which heals the injuries caused by mistakes, misunderstandings, and disputes. And let us ask him for the grace to send us forth, in humility and meekness, along the demanding but enriching path of seeking peace.[3]

The Holy Father's words bring to mind the day I visited the Jordan River with my group of journalists. It was hot and sunny, with barely any breeze. We meandered through the busy visitor's center, and then down to the shore. The river was perfectly still, and the riverbanks were lined with trees and lush flora. A band of tourists in white robes were waiting at a shaded area downriver. They were waiting to be baptized—a popular custom among pilgrims to the Holy Land.

Across the river from us was the place traditionally held to be Jesus' baptismal site. Pope Francis would visit the spot later that same day, and so the entire area had been closed off. But I didn't need to see the exact place for myself in order to get an idea of what Jesus' baptism might have been like. I was at the same river—that itself was an incredible gift.

I could almost see John the Baptist, standing in waist-deep water, motioning for the people to come forward. He lowers each one gently into the water, and then raises them back up, dripping wet and ever so joyful. Just as he reaches for the next penitent, a man approaches the river and quietly stands on the bank. John sees him and stops mid-baptism, with a look of amazement coming across his face. It's the Messiah!

Jesus is seeking baptism, but John resists because he knows Jesus has no need of it. Jesus tells him, "Allow it now, for thus it is fitting for us to fulfill all righteousness (Mt 3:15)."

Until I saw the Jordan River for myself, I'd supposed that the most awesome part of Jesus' baptism was the fact that he—the Son of God—humbled himself to be baptized. He'd come to baptize others in the Spirit, yet he sought baptism for himself because he wanted to live in perfect accordance with God's law.

Even better was what came next in the narrative:

> On coming up out of the water he saw the heavens being torn open and the Spirit, like a dove, descending upon him. And a voice came from the heavens, "You are my beloved Son; with you I am well pleased." (Mk 1:10–11)

I looked up at the sky and tried to "see" the heavens opening and the dove descending. The white-robed tourists downriver helped me to imagine the many people who had come to be baptized by John. They witnessed the heavens open, and saw the dove appear. They heard the voice from heaven proclaiming, "You are my beloved Son; with you I am well pleased." They came to find a better way.

Had they come to escape some form of injustice?

Along the stillness and beauty of the Jordan River, the Father revealed his extraordinary love for his Son, and from then on, it would be known to all generations. I'd heard or read that Gospel passage so many times before, but never before had I understood what it fully meant.

Here's something even more remarkable to take into account. There are rarely clouds in Israel. In fact, I didn't see a single cloud the entire ten days I was there. So, what exactly was it that opened when Jesus was baptized? I wondered what the miracle looked like, and marveled at God's power. If he can "open" the sky over Israel, he can release us from injustice.

Viewing Our Interior Landscape

What injustice burdens you? Have you been discriminated against because of your culture or religion? Perhaps it was something subtle, like a snide remark whispered behind your back, or the withholding of some privilege. That can be painful and disturbing.

Or perhaps you have suffered a deeper, more arbitrary form of injustice: Perhaps you were fired from your job without good reason, suddenly and without recourse, leaving you high and dry and without resources. Or maybe an auto accident or sudden illness left you or a loved one disabled. Coping with such things can leave you distressed and exhausted.

Perhaps, despite your best efforts, you've been abandoned, or lost something or someone precious to you. The heartbreak can consume you and cause lingering anguish. Injustice, no matter how it comes about, can be a bitter pill to swallow.

Injustice becomes a knot that can trap us in sinfulness and turn us away from God. We can become caustic and vengeful. Revenge can lead us to hatred, and that's a serious sin. Sometimes, people who suffer injustice let their anger incite them to violence and destruction. Once we've stepped down that path, it's hard to turn back.

That's why we need to turn our knot of injustice over to Our Lady, Undoer of Knots—before it entangles us in sin and ruin. We might prefer to cling to the knot, seeking vengeance or believing we deserve restitution.

And yet, God knows better.

He knows whether we need restitution, and he knows best how to handle the people who have treated us unjustly. We don't need to seek revenge; we need to surrender the knot of injustice to Our Lady. She will know exactly how to undo it, if only we give it to her freely.

The Journey Begins: Let Us Pray for the Gift of True Justice

Our Lady, Undoer of Knots,

The injustice I bear infuriates me. I don't want to surrender it; I want to avenge it. I want what I believe I deserve. I want the perpetrator of the injustice to make amends. I want to take matters into my own hands and set things right. That might not be the godly way of doing things, but it's the way I'd prefer to do them.

Mother, help me to turn away from my sinfulness and toward God. Take this knot of injustice from me [name the knot] and hold it fast in your hands so that I won't be able to take it back. Work on it with all your love and diligence so that it becomes a source of grace and growth rather than a source of anger and resentment.

> You know that it's difficult for me to forgive and let go. Pray for me, please, and lead me to forgiveness and confidence in God's wisdom and mercy. Show me that God can handle this far better than I can, and help me to have faith and trust in him to do just that. Pray for me, that God would instill in me true justice, the ability to seek not my rights but his will in all things.
>
> Dear Lady, along with the knot itself, I place into your hands those who have been unjust to me and any others affected by their actions. Guide them to repentance and conversion of heart.
>
> Mother, pray for me and for all who bear the burden of injustice. I also want to unite my prayers with those of Pope Francis, asking that lasting peace may be granted to the Holy Land. Amen.

Pray the Rosary, offering it in petition for those who have been unjust to you, and others who have suffered injustice. Pray also for peace in the Holy Land. (Additional information on how to pray the Rosary can be found on pages 125–129.)

Stepping Out in Faith

Take some time to think about the questions below. Then answer them as honestly as you can so that your heart can continue to grow more and more peaceful.

- What injustice do you bear? How did it come about?
- What is it, specifically, that hurts you most about it? Why?
- What have you learned from this experience?
- If you could explain your feelings to the person(s) causing the injustice, what would you say? Tell this to Our Lady and let her lift the pain and anger from your heart.

Make a concrete resolution to take one step toward peace in your heart today.

Day Two: Wall of Bethlehem

The Knot of Separation

> The divisions among Christians, while they hurt the Church, they wound Christ. And, divided, we wound Christ. The Church is indeed the body in which Christ is the head. We know well how much Jesus cared that his disciples remain united in His love.
>
> —Pope Francis[1]

Can you think of a time when you felt the pain of being separated from a friend or loved one? At one time or another, most of us have had such an experience. You may even be experiencing it right now, and are hoping that this little book will guide you along a more peaceful path. Rest assured, Our Lady wants this, too. She wants you to place your troubles into her lap, with confidence and childlike trust.

Knots of separation have many different causes. Perhaps you've experienced some kind of social or professional "disconnection." Or maybe you've felt the knot of estrangement from a loved one over a stubbornly held grudge. The knot snarls both ways: someone does something of which the other party disapproved, or doesn't do something the other expected. Whether the action was intentional or accidental, the knot remains until someone chooses to release it.

Some knots are formed through embarrassment or a sense of failure; others spring up out of anger, because someone refuses to forgive. Frustration, ignorance, misunderstanding, pride—all these things create divisions that form small, yet unmistakable knots in the cords of our lives.

Of course, some kinds of separation are regrettable, but necessary. We may need to set boundaries with coworkers or acquaintances to protect those we cherish. If someone is being abusive or manipulative, even within our own families, we may need to create a healthy space to protect ourselves or our loved ones. We must treat everyone charitably, and pray for their healing and conversion. And yet, sometimes that is easiest to accomplish when we don't spend a lot of time in their presence.

Even so, separation can be painful, and the devil will do everything possible to feed feelings of resentment and anger in order to widen the breach as much as possible, far more than is needed. During these times, we need our Blessed Mother to work to unbind the knots that have caused the sinfulness and division. Through her intercession, we can find healing and peace, even in the most difficult of situations.

Is there a knot separating you from a brother or sister, a wall that needs to come down? Working things out requires humility and can take a lot of effort, effort that we may not want to expend. It becomes easier to separate ourselves so that we don't have to deal with it; we think it will make us feel more secure. In actuality, just the opposite is true: these walls become a constant reminder that there is something on the other side that we need to avoid or fear. Walls tend to create more problems than they resolve. Walls of separation are blockades that stop people from relating to each other, in much the same way that the knots they cause in our lives block our way to holiness.

Signs from the Holy Land: The Walls Mary Knew

I was reminded of the knots of separation in my own life as I observed what happened when Pope Francis journeyed to Bethlehem. First landing by helicopter in the Palestinian state, he followed the same footsteps that millions of pilgrims throughout the centuries and from all over the world had traveled in order to pray at the birthplace of the Savior. After leaving the helicopter, the pope greeted Palestinian President Mahmoud Abbas, pleading with him to be brave in the quest for peace between Palestine and Israel.

The Holy Father said, "The time has come for everyone to find the courage to be generous and creative in the service of the common good."[2]

On his way by car to the Church of the Nativity, Pope Francis made a surprise stop at the separation wall that divides Palestine and Israel and surrounds Bethlehem on three sides—one of the most defining moments of his Holy Land pilgrimage. He got out of the car, walked to the wall, and solemnly leaned his head and hand against it. In stillness, he prayed there for four minutes before returning to the car and proceeding to Manger Square.

No one knows for sure what Pope Francis prayed during those four minutes, but I certainly can imagine that it included a fervent petition for peace and for the dividing walls to be torn down once and for all. "Courage" and "peace" became a theme for the pontiff's visit to Bethlehem, and I know it should be a theme in my own life as well. During his public addresses there, he used the word "peace" twelve times and the word "courage" four times. Clearly, his heart was heavy, yearning for a peaceful and permanent resolution to the conflict.

I was deeply touched by the Holy Father's gesture, as was the rest of the world. It made me ask myself how many times I have stopped at my own wall of separation to reflect on my failures toward peace and to pray for a way to tear down the wall.

Consider the words of the Holy Father spoken in Bethlehem:

> For decades the Middle East has known the tragic consequences of a protracted conflict which has inflicted many wounds so difficult to heal. . . . Even in the absence of violence, the climate of instability and a lack of mutual understanding have produced insecurity, the violation of rights, isolation, and the flight of entire communities, conflicts, shortages, and sufferings of every sort.[3]

Separation inflicts wounds that are difficult to heal.

When I first saw the separation wall for myself, I was struck by how similar the two sides of the city appeared to be on each side of the wall's expanse. I'd naïvely expected that there would be a visible difference between the Israeli and Palestinian sides because of the differences in their political and territorial viewpoints. The wall was foreboding and, frankly, depressing. Spanning 430 miles, it consists of concrete walls three times the height of a man, barbed wire, other barriers, and guard towers. Military checkpoints ensure that no one comes or goes without permission. It is formidable, to say the least.

At the wall, my companions and I left our van and Israeli tour guide behind, passed through the checkpoint, boarded a bus, and were led by a Palestinian tour guide through Bethlehem. I looked back at our Israeli tour guide, then at the wall, and then at our Palestinian tour guide. Both men were kind and knowledgeable; both loved their people and heritage. How could it be that they both lived in the midst of such conflict? They were persons—just like me—with homes, families, friends, goals, and dreams. Yet they lived amidst separation. So do I. So do you.

And so we turn to Mary, the great unifier and undoer of knots. She understands the walls of separation that exist between people and nations. Such walls existed long before her own time. Her main task is to lead us closer to her son, Jesus, and to transform the knotted ribbon of our lives into one that is smooth and grace-filled, a cord that binds us to the Sacred Heart of Jesus.

When Mary gave birth to Jesus in Bethlehem more than two thousand years ago, she was surrounded by walls of separation. They weren't walls in the literal sense, but rather walls that separated the Jewish people from the freedom they both longed for and deserved. Palestine, as well as the rest of Judea, was under Roman occupation in the Holy Family's time. Their land belonged to Caesar. The Jewish people no longer governed themselves; rather, they were governed by Herod the Great, a king appointed by Caesar.

Roman soldiers wandered the towns and roads—a stark reminder of the freedom lost. They could earn money for their families, but they had to pay high taxes that kept them in poverty. The walls of separation that touched the lives of Joseph, Mary, and Jesus most profoundly were those that separated the Jews as the people they used to be from the people they had become. They were subject to the whims and wishes of Caesar and Herod, and at times, they were victims of the Roman soldiers' brutality. Their walls of separation were invisible yet real.

And so, Mary is compassionate toward our pain of separation, not only because she loves us, but also because she has experienced such separation herself. She was proud of her Jewish heritage, as we know from the Magnificat, and so it must have been painful for her to witness the poverty and oppression of her people. Rather than give birth in the comfort of her own home, she was forced to give birth on the road, in Bethlehem. Along with the rest of Judea, the Holy Family had been forced to travel to their city of origin in order to be counted. Caesar wanted to know just how many Jews he had under his thumb. In spite of Mary's advanced pregnancy, she and Joseph had to pack a few necessities and head off to Bethlehem. Either on donkey or foot, they made the eighty-mile journey over rugged territory. Though she herself was sinless, Mary suffered under the sinfulness of others. The devil—the great divider—touched her life as he touches ours.

Viewing Our Interior Landscape

Pope Francis's words to the leaders of Palestine and Israel apply to us as well. They apply not just in regard to political, territorial, or religious conflict, but also to knots in our lives that come from separated relationships as well. These walls of separation that we face divide us as surely as the walls that divided the Jews and the Romans, and that now divide the Palestinians and the Israelis. They may have a different purpose, but they cause as much pain.

The Holy Father tells us, "The time has come for everyone to find the courage to be generous and creative in the service of the common good."[4] Our Lady, Undoer of Knots, can help us to find the courage we need to be generous and creative as she gently undoes the knots of separation in our lives.

Are you enduring a knot of separation that needs to be undone? Perhaps you've had a falling-out with a loved one, or one of your children is estranged from the family. That's painful, not only because of the separation itself, but also because of the turmoil it causes inside of us. Do you have a friend or family member who is deployed with the military? Not only can this steep us in loneliness, but we must also deal with constant fears about his or her safety. Are you or your spouse separated from family members because of past abuse or neglect, so that it is necessary to put a wall of protection between you? Is there an emotional divide between you and family members who think far differently from you, or who are hostile toward your principles and beliefs? There are countless ways we can be experiencing separation, and they are all miserable to endure.

Our Lady, Undoer of Knots, understands about walls that separate, and she understands our sadness and suffering. She wants to tear down our walls of separation and replace them with love and freedom. Her heart is open to us, drawing us in with her motherly care. For that to happen, we must actually want the walls to come down and that requires God's grace. We must pray for the desire to breach the walls and extend our hand in Christian charity toward the other. Likewise, we must pray that those who are separated from us receive the same graces as well.

If we ask in sincerity, Our Lady, Undoer of Knots, will intercede for us and the knot of separation in our lives will become untied in her hands. She wants this for us with all her Immaculate Heart.

The Journey Begins: Let Us Pray for the Gift of True Unity

Our Lady, Undoer of Knots,

You are a powerful intercessor before the Triune God, and you are truly my Mother. You care about every aspect of my life; the walls of separation that hurt me, hurt you, too, because I am your child and you love me. You care also about those from whom I have separated myself because they also are your children.

You see my heart because your closeness to God allows you to see deep inside of me. You know the people I struggle with, and you know everything that divides us. Please ask your Son to forgive me for all that I have done to build these walls. So too, please forgive, and ask your Son to forgive, those who have built walls that keep me out. I know that these walls are sinful, and I am sorry.

Take this knot into your loving hands and work diligently to untie it. Loosen the snarls of misunderstanding, instability, and conflict. Give me courage and a sincere desire for peace in my life. Then show me the steps I should take to make this peace a reality, that I might experience the gift of true unity with all those you love, and those who love God.

> Mother, I also pray for those who are separated by actual walls—those in the Middle East who live behind walls that separate and who suffer from the consequences. I want to unite my prayers with those of Pope Francis, asking God to fell the walls and grant lasting peace to the Holy Land. Amen.

Pray the Rosary, offering it for those from whom you are separated by walls of your or their making. Pray also for peace in the Holy Land.

Stepping Out in Faith

Take some time to think about the questions below. Then answer them as honestly as you can so that your heart can continue to grow more and more peaceful.

- From whom are you separated?
- How did it happen? How might you have contributed to the division?
- What needs to happen for the wall to begin coming down?
- What's kept you from taking those steps until now?
- What little change can you make in your attitude that will start the process?

Make a concrete resolution to take one step toward peace in your heart today.

Day Three: Grotto of the Nativity

The Knot of Confusion

> The one who trusts in himself, in his own richness or ideologies, is destined for unhappiness. The one who trusts in the Lord, on the other hand, bears fruit even in time of drought.
>
> —Pope Francis[1]

The doctors of the Law—those who had structured it and knew Jewish Law inside and out—rejected Jesus and his message of a new covenant. They thought they had everything figured out: what was and what wasn't acceptable, and just how each person's life should go. They knew everything, and then this man named Jesus came along and caused confusion. He had a new way of thinking, praying, and being. He messed with their system, and they wanted none of it. In fact, they weren't only closed to Jesus' message, but they hated him and wanted to put him to death.

No one likes to be confused, to have our status quo shaken. Once we have things figured out, we want to be left to our own devices to make certain that everything happens according to our own private convictions. We'd prefer to tell God how our lives should go rather than listen to him tell us the way it should be. Confusion disturbs the peace in our hearts and minds. It disturbs the peace we think we've achieved when things seem to be going our way. So, we close ourselves to God's will and his message for us. We haven't the time or tolerance for confusion of any kind.

Yet, confusing things happen to us every day. A financial setback can prevent us from achieving long-anticipated personal goals. A harsh dose of reality can uproot cherished beliefs and ideals, cause us to doubt even those closest to us, leaving us grappling for truth or reassurance. When this confusion stems from our own choices, it can be difficult enough. It can be even worse when we're challenged by confusion that stems from the actions and choices of other people, leaving us feeling utterly perplexed and powerless.

Even in these times, though, Our Lady shows us the way to undo these knots of confusion and rediscover the way of peace.

Signs from the Holy Land: A Child Shall Lead Them

During his time in Palestine, Pope Francis met with the president and local authorities. He celebrated Mass, prayed the *Regina Coeli* with a crowd of ten thousand people in Manger Square, and visited the Grotto of the Nativity. But two other stops in his itinerary showed his compassion for Palestinian families—lunch with a group of families at the Franciscan convent, Casa Nova, and a visit with the children of the Dheisheh Refugee Camp.

In the Book of Isaiah, the prophet spoke of one who would come to restore the lost. "A little child [shall] lead them" (Is 11:6), he predicted. In times of chaos and confusion, the innocence and candor of young children can greatly simplify the issues at stake, helping us to see that which is most important, most essential. I was reminded of this as I watched Pope Francis from a distance during his day in Bethlehem, the birthplace of *the* child, our Lord Jesus. No doubt Pope Francis made this connection as he stopped to spend time with the Palestinian children who became refugees as a result of the conflict that has plagued their state.

I wonder if the Palestinian people sometimes feel confused. There are frequent disputes with Israel over rights and territories that even lead to outbreaks of violence. I shared some of that confusion as our guide tried to explain the segregated bus lines—one for Palestinians, one for Arabs, and one for Israelis.

What's more, many Palestinians live meagerly; they can't find jobs that will support their families. Most young people leave, and those who are left—young and old alike—depend mostly on tourism to survive. The outbreaks of violence have caused a dwindling of the tourism trade, threatening their livelihood. At Dheisheh, the plight of the refugee children—robbed of family, home, and security—testified to the collateral damage of this ongoing conflict.

Pope Francis's words to Palestinian President Mahmoud Abbas earlier that day seem to echo what must have been on his heart while visiting the birthplace of our Savior and the refugee children:

> . . . I can only express my profound hope that all will refrain from initiatives and actions which contradict the stated desire to reach a true agreement, and that peace will be pursued with tireless determination and tenacity. Peace will bring countless benefits for the peoples of this region and for the world as a whole. And so it must resolutely be pursued, even if each side has to make certain sacrifices.[2]

The day my group went to Bethlehem, there was a great deal of security—not because of the pope's visit two days prior, but because on the previous night there had been a fire in the Grotto of the Nativity, significantly damaging the walls and ornamentation. I was grateful that the site had not been demolished, yet shaken by the confusing rumors about the cause of the fire—some suggested that it was arson. Who would set fire to the birthplace of Jesus? Why would they do such a thing? Much to everyone's relief, it was discovered that the fire had started accidentally when one of the lanterns had fallen and the materials in the vicinity caught flame.

The Emperor Justinian built the Church of the Nativity, now badly in need of repair, in AD 530, over the cave in which Jesus was born—a reconstruction of the first church, built by Constantine and St. Helena and consecrated in AD 339. The only way to enter the church is through the Door of Humility, a tiny rectangular passageway that made even me, at five-foot-two, have to duck. It was built during Ottoman times to prevent looters from driving their carts in and out. The ownership of the tiny church was a source of ongoing dispute, passing alternately from the hands of the Persians, Muslims, Crusaders, Mamluk, and the Ottomans. In 1852, it was put in the shared custody of the Roman Catholic, Armenian, and Greek Orthodox Churches.

As I stood there in the grotto, all of the Christmas cards I'd ever seen flashed before my eyes. For all their beauty and charm, none came close to the magnificence and holiness of this place. No Christmas pageant, Midnight Mass, or concert could match it. There was nothing in the world remotely like standing at the site of the Nativity. I was gripped by its age and history, and marveled over the fact that it had changed hands so many times over the centuries, yet remained standing.

The Grotto of the Nativity lies below the sanctuary, and even though I couldn't see it, I could feel it. My stomach actually quivered (just a bit) and my heart pounded with . . . what? Excitement? Awe? Whatever it was, it was overwhelming in the most amazing way. There, truly beneath my feet, was the birthplace of the Redeemer of the World: my Redeemer and King.

As I contemplated the bronze star that marked the spot where Jesus was born, I thought about Mary, and what it might have been like to give birth to the Son of God in nothing more than a space carved into the rock. I pondered the Annunciation, and how she might have responded to the Angel Gabriel's approach. We'd seen the Grotto of the Annunciation earlier in the trip, and I was astounded at its simplicity. It, too, was just a stark hole, far smaller than I'd expected, carved into the rock. How incredible, I thought to myself, that our Lord was conceived, born, and buried in the same environment: a small, dark hollow in the side of a mount of hardened earth.

Mary was there with Jesus at all three events. She had witnessed the three most important miracles—and possibly the most confusing, for eyewitnesses—known to mankind.

When Gabriel appeared to Mary, she was surprised at his greeting, perplexed at his request. She'd taken a vow of virginity. How would it be possible for her to conceive and bear any son, much less the Son of God? And when that Son was born, what must have gone on in her mind and her heart as she sat, holding Jesus and knowing that he had come from her womb—the womb of a human—and yet was God? She saw him die on the cross, she held his dead, tortured body, and she herself helped to lay him in the tomb. How could it be that after three days he rose from the dead?

Mary had tremendous faith, but I believe she still must have faced much confusion in her life. We have some evidence of this in scripture:

> And coming to her, he said, "Hail, favored one! The Lord is with you." But she was greatly troubled at what was said and pondered what sort of greeting this might be. Then the angel said to her, "Do not be afraid, Mary, for you have found favor with God. Behold, you will conceive in your womb and bear a son, and you shall name him

> Jesus. He will be great and will be called Son of the Most High, and the Lord God will give him the throne of David his father, and he will rule over the house of Jacob forever, and of his kingdom there will be no end." But Mary said to the angel, "How can this be, since I have no relations with a man?" (Lk 1:28–34)

Yes, Mary was "greatly troubled" by the angel's words, and "pondered what sort of greeting it might be." Yet, she didn't counter it; she accepted it in spite of the confusion it stirred within her. And when Gabriel spoke even more confusing words—his request that she agree to become the Mother of God—she did not scoff. Because of the vow she had taken, a pregnancy in human terms was simply not possible. Yet she reacted in humility and asked one simple question: "How can this be?"

Viewing Our Interior Landscape

It can be as difficult for us to face the confusion in our lives as it was for Mary to face the confusion in hers. Born without the consequences of original sin, she was gifted with perfect reason. Even so, it took great humility to work through the confusing circumstances of her life, choosing daily to put her faith and trust in God.

Mary understands our confusion, and understands that our reasoning is imperfect. She understands us because we're her children. She knows how we got into the state of confusion, and she knows how to get us out. When consuming knots of confusion overtake us, Our Lady, Undoer of Knots, stands ready to help. Her able hands can take up our knots of confusion, unknot them, and turn them into something beautiful and fruitful.

What's the source of your confusion? Do you have a loved one involved in risk-taking behavior like crime or addiction? It can be confusing to try to help them. Perhaps you're facing an ethical dilemma that's blurring the proper course of action. Maybe you have a family member who has been diagnosed with an irreversible and life-threatening condition. You might be challenged by end-of-life decisions for an aging parent. All of these situations can be not only confusing, but downright scary.

When we are confused by the words and actions (or inaction, as the case may be) of others, we can also turn them over to the Blessed Mother, who loves us all. When we entrust the situation to her, she gladly takes all of us into her arms and begins immediately to tackle the knots that are causing confusion in us and perpetrating confusion in others.

Just give those knots unreservedly over to her. Don't take them back, to try to stew over them or to take matters into your own hands. That will do more harm than good.

The Journey Begins: Let Us Pray for the Gift of Humble Trust

Our Lady, Undoer of Knots,

You faced confusion in your life and yet didn't let it overwhelm you. When the Angel Gabriel greeted you with words that were strange to you, you carefully took them in and pondered them. When he asked you to become the Mother of God, you needed to know only one thing—how was it to happen. You accepted not only the conception and birth of Jesus, but also his death and resurrection—all with humility, trust, and faith.

Because you are my Mother, I know you truly understand my confusion. You know what this confusion [name the knot] costs me, and you know what needs to be done in order to resolve it. You also understand the confusion of the others in my life (mention by name), for you are their Mother, too. You know what it costs them and what needs to be done for its resolution.

Mother, implore your son for mercy and forgiveness for any sinful choices caught up in these knots. Pray for me, that I might move from confusion to humility and trust in the loving hand of God. Please work diligently to undo the knots so that order might be restored in the hearts and minds of all involved. Our Lady, Undoer of Knots, I beg you to save me from this confusion.

> Mother, I also pray for those who are steeped in confusion by the conflict in the Middle East and who suffer from its consequences. I want to unite my prayers with those of Pope Francis, asking God to dispel the confusion and grant lasting peace to the Holy Land. Amen.

Pray the Rosary, offering it in petition for a resolution to the confusion in your life. Pray also for peace in the Holy Land.

Stepping Out in Faith

Take some time to think about the questions below. Then answer them as honestly as you can so that your heart can continue to grow more and more peaceful.

- What kind of confusion do you face in your life right now?
- How did it come about? What factors contributed to it?
- What would it take for the confusion to be resolved?
- What has prohibited you so far from seeking a resolution?
- Practically speaking, what part might you play in a resolution?

Make a concrete resolution to take one step toward peace in your heart today.

Day Four: Mount of Olives

The Knot of Hopelessness

> May the Church be a place of God's mercy and hope, where all feel welcomed, loved, forgiven and encouraged to live according to the good life of the Gospel. And to make others feel welcomed, loved, forgiven and encouraged, the Church must be with doors wide open so that all may enter. And we must go out through these doors and proclaim the Gospel.
>
> —Pope Francis[1]

We use the word *hope* a lot in our day-to-day conversations:

- "I hope I get that job."
- "My hope is that we'll be able to sell our house within six months."
- "Here's hoping!"
- "I should hope so."

We use it in many ways to express what we'd like to receive or see happen.

We use hope in a negative way, as well:

- "That's a hopeless case."
- "There's no hope left, we've tried all our options."
- "It's no use hoping he'll change. He'll always be that way."
- "I've been disappointed so many times; I don't even want to hope anymore."

When we can't visualize the end result, we declare that there's "no hope."

Most of us use hope in the context of wanting something to happen—or not happen, as the case may be. We could just as well use the word *wish* instead. "I wish things were different." "I wish I was rich." "I wish he wouldn't do that." On the surface, that kind of thinking is harmless. We're expressing our preference. But there's a deeper, more serious meaning of hope. Real hope has to do with our trust and faith in God and our sincere desire for salvation.

The *Catechism of the Catholic Church* explains it this way:

> The virtue of hope responds to the aspiration to happiness which God has placed in the heart of every man; it takes up the hopes that inspire men's activities and purifies them so as to order them to the Kingdom of heaven; it keeps man from discouragement; it sustains him during times of abandonment; it opens up his heart in expectation of eternal beatitude. Buoyed up by hope, he is preserved from selfishness and led to the happiness that flows from charity. (CCC 1818)

We can *hope*, and then we can *have hope*. It seems like the exact same thing, but it's not. When we don't get what we've hoped for, we can become discouraged, even irritated or angry. Usually, that's temporary. But sometimes that discouragement, irritation, or anger gets out of hand, and we fall into despair. When we despair, we turn away from God. We stop trusting him, lose our faith in him, and con ourselves into believing that he no longer cares about our needs, or even that he cares about us personally.

In extreme cases, we might even be tempted to lose hope completely. So convinced that our sins are unforgiveable, and that we ourselves are unlovable, we no longer hope in heaven or anticipate our God will save us. To lose hope completely in this way is to despair, which is contrary to God's goodness, justice, mercy, and faithfulness.

To give in to despair is a serious sin, for it involves turning our backs on God and deliberately choosing the lie of the evil one over the truth of what God has revealed: You are not hopeless. You are a most beloved child of God.

No one intentionally sets out toward hopelessness. It happens incrementally, so imperceptibly that often the severity goes unnoticed until something happens that stops us short and we feel the knot that has us hopelessly bound. For example, after a lifetime of faith and trust, you find that suddenly the most precious thing in the world to you has been taken away: perhaps you have lost a spouse or other loved one, or have experienced some other crushing loss. It may be that you are struggling to right yourself after experiencing such upheaval, or are suffering from depression, anxiety, or another mental disorder.

Perhaps your loss is compounded by a sense of guilt or shame, be it a recent misjudgment or something that happened years ago, some regret you've never been able to shake and that you are certain is the cause for all your trouble. Some dark corner of your past still has its grip on you, leaving you feeling unworthy of forgiveness. Things haven't turned out at all the way you'd anticipated.

Signs from the Holy Land: In the Garden

In the Church of All Nations on the Mount of Olives in Jerusalem, Pope Francis celebrated Mass with hundreds of priests, seminarians, and religious living in the Holy Land. The church's official name is the Basilica of the Agony because it is next to the Garden of Gethsemane and enshrines a section of the stone on which Jesus prayed just before he was arrested. The modern church was completed in 1924 and is built on the foundations of a fourth-century Byzantine basilica and a twelfth-century crusader chapel. The name Church of All Nations comes from the fact that twelve different countries helped to fund its construction.

The Holy Father had arrived at the church immediately following a private meeting with the Ecumenical Patriarch of Constantinople, Bartholomew. He was greeted with cheers and applause, and it was clear that the enthusiasm was mutual. The pope was radiant with joy as he made his way down the center aisle, shaking hands, giving pats on the shoulder, and waving to those he could not reach. But his joy turned to solemnness as he stood before the altar, under which lay the piece of stone upon which our Lord suffered his agony. After standing briefly, he prostrated himself and reverently kissed the sacred stone. Then he rose and proceeded to prepare for holy Mass.

During his homily, Pope Francis spoke humbly and frankly about Jesus' deadly anguish, and the need to ask ourselves, "Who am I, before the sufferings of my Lord?" He spoke also about Jesus' faithfulness and our need to follow him with trust, despite our weaknesses, failures, and betrayals. He pointed out that Jesus had asked his disciples to stay and pray with him, but they were "overcome with doubt, weariness, and fright." But then Pope Francis assured them of the Lord's goodness and mercy. He gave them hope:

> We are all exposed to sin, to evil, to betrayal. . . . We are fully conscious of the disproportion between the grandeur of God's call and of own littleness, between the sublimity of the mission and the reality of our human weakness. Yet the Lord in his great goodness and his infinite mercy always takes us by the hand lest we drown in the sea of our fears and anxieties. He is ever at our side, he never abandons us. And so, let us not be overwhelmed by fear or disheartened, but with courage and confidence let us press forward in our journey and in our mission.[2]

The day we visited the Garden of Gethsemane, it was sunny and bright. It was an absolutely beautiful day, the kind that makes you feel happy and carefree. The lovely weather and lush garden were a drastic contrast to the scene of the Agony—dark, gloomy, and tragic. Here in this garden, men perspire because of an act of God (baking under Israel's unrelenting sunshine and sultry winds), where centuries before, God sweat blood because of the actions of man—eating the forbidden fruit and unleashing a long litany of sin and death.

The guide pointed to an ancient olive tree in the middle of the garden, a tree old enough to have witnessed the night Jesus went there with his disciples. Had one or another of the disciples leaned against it while waiting for Jesus to finish praying?

I closed my eyes and reenacted the sequence of events in my imagination—a stroll from the Upper Room to the Mount of Olives after the Last Supper, our Lord with the prospect of the cross already weighing heavily upon his shoulders, and the disciples unwittingly sauntering along. Perhaps a few of them noticed Jesus' somber demeanor, but did they even have a clue as to why?

I imagined the disciples dozing off under the tree, rousing momentarily at Jesus' invitation to prayer before going back to sleep.

I saw Jesus praying alone, begging for the cup to pass him by as the angel brought him solace in his affliction so extreme, drops of blood fell to the ground.

I heard the soldiers marching in, then scuffling, and then dragging Jesus off to prison, torment, torture, and death. Yes, I could see it, and I also could feel it.

The seventy-two hours following the Last Supper had to be ones of utter hopelessness for the disciples. Their mentor, friend, and hero—the man they'd left everything and everyone to follow—had been taken prisoner by Pontius Pilate's soldiers. Surely they knew that the consequences would be grave. Overcome by fear and hopelessness, they fled—all but one. John alone stayed near to Jesus.

Peter, the Rock upon whom Jesus was to build his Church, denied his Lord three times. Judas Iscariot committed suicide, certain that he would never be forgiven for betraying Jesus to the Pharisees. The disciples had seen Jesus with their own eyes, touched him with their own hands, and heard him with their own ears . . . and still they lost hope when their world was turned upside down.

We have much in common with the disciples. We can find ourselves in the scuffle in the Garden of Gethsemane, not understanding what's going on or what to do next. When we're facing desperate situations and grave consequences, we become overcome with fear and hopelessness, and flee mentally, emotionally, and spiritually and sometimes in actuality. We end up denying our Lord or betraying him entirely. We convince ourselves that our sins are unforgiveable. We might even contemplate suicide. Everything becomes gnarled and knotted and we find ourselves ensnared in the knot of hopelessness.

Viewing Our Interior Landscape

When we're knotted in hopelessness, we must turn to Our Lady, Undoer of Knots. There is no knot that's too hopeless for her to undo. She felt the anguish of any mother unable to stop her child's torment. She witnessed the hopelessness of the disciples after Jesus' arrest. She's known the hopelessness of her children throughout time, and she knows your hopelessness right now. What's more, she knows how to untie the knots of hopelessness.

Mary is waiting for us to hand over our knots of hopelessness to her. She wants them, truly, so that she can undo them and set us free from them. She realizes how serious hopelessness can be and how it can damage our relationship with her son, and she doesn't want that to happen.

Dealing with hopelessness can be tricky, though, because we can be so steeped in it that we lose our desire to seek help. Hopelessness can become a kind of defense mechanism—it feels safer not to hope because hoping might lead to disappointment, and we don't want to be disappointed. So, if we don't hope, we'll never be disappointed. But hopelessness is never safer; it's actually risky, because we risk missing out on witnessing God's goodness, justice, mercy, and faithfulness in our lives and the lives of others. Blind hope brings disappointment; hope in God brings fulfillment. If we're afraid to hope, we must ask Our Lady, Undoer of Knots, to pray for us and to give us the grace to want to be helped out of our hopelessness.

Do you think your situation is hopeless? Are you struggling with a chronic illness, or an unrelenting burden of circumstance? Are you suffering from anxiety or depression that is wreaking havoc in your personal life? Take it to Mary (and consider discussing it with your doctor as well). Have you committed a serious sin like having an abortion or committing adultery? Although serious, these are not unforgiveable sins. Yet it can be hard to believe we're loved and forgiven; we can carry the guilt with us for a lifetime. Perhaps you've missed out on an amazing opportunity—not just once, but many times—and feel like throwing in the towel. Whether it's one, a combination of any or all of these heartbreaks, or something entirely different, hopelessness can be all-consuming and sometimes even debilitating.

The most tangible experience of hopelessness I experienced in the Holy Land was at Masada, a mountain-top fortress built in 30 BC by King Herod. Masada contains Herod's palace, as well as bathhouses, watchtowers, storerooms, and a synagogue.[3] It's virtually an entire city built on the flat top of a mountain. It overlooks the desert to the west and the Dead Sea to the east; the view is breathtaking. Its steep sides rise 1,300 feet above the ground—far, far too high for my acrophobia. Still, I felt driven to ride the cable car to the top and take part in the tour along with my companions. They knew of my fear, and literally stood guard around me during the excursion so that I wouldn't panic.

I'm glad I went. The history of Masada is one of courage and heroism, and as our guide related the story, I began to see what real hopelessness can be. Masada was conquered by zealots at the rise of the Jewish revolt against the Romans in 68 BC. In AD 72, the Romans besieged Masada, constructing a huge earthen ramp on the fortress's west side. The zealots, including women and children, were trapped with no way to get reinforcements or supplies. Knowing the brutality of the Roman military, the zealots expected that they would be killed, their wives raped, and their children enslaved. There seemed no way out. In AD 73, rather than succumb to Roman capture the 960 zealots decided first to kill their wives and children and then themselves.

Standing atop Masada and gazing down at the Roman structures below, I could feel the utter hopelessness of the Jewish zealots. What must have it been like for them? I thought of the times in my life during which I'd felt hopelessness, but none of them compared to what I imagined the Jews had experienced. At that moment, I realized how blessed I really am—to have my faith to lean on and my Mother Mary to flee to whenever I start running out of hope.

Whenever we feel ourselves running out of hope, it's time to flee to Our Lady, Undoer of Knots. When we release our burden to her prayerfully and deliberately, and with resolve to let go of the knots completely, we'll be blessed with the freedom to heal and find new courage. This isn't a one-time thing, however. We will probably need to do it many times until we can truly and finally let go of the hopelessness. What's more, it gives Mary the freedom to work on the knot without our interference. She'll let us know if there's something specific for us to do. In the meantime, we can be assured that Our Lady, Undoer of Knots, is in charge.

The Journey Begins: Let Us Pray for the Gift of Hope

Our Lady, Undoer of Knots,

Please help me out of my hopelessness. From my human perspective, I see no way out. But, God, who knows everything, knows the way out. He has the power to fix whatever it is that's caused this hopeless situation, to forgive my sinfulness, and to change my battered heart.

Mary, you also know the way out because God gives you the special grace of understanding the concerns of your children. Even in my hopelessness, I am your child. You understand what I'm going through, and you understand why things are the way they are. Show me, somehow, that you are there for me. Assure me that there is reason to hope and protect me from despair.

Mother, you are waiting for me to hand over this knot to you, this knot of [name the knot].

Deep down, I want to turn it completely over to you, but I'm afraid to do so. My fearfulness keeps me from truly hoping. My sinfulness keeps me from completely trusting in God's goodness, justice, mercy, and faithfulness. I'm caught in this knot that needs your hands to lovingly undo.

Our Lady, Undoer of Knots, please take this knot from me and begin working on it immediately. If I try to snatch it back, gently remind me that it's better off in your hands than mine. As you work, intercede for me to your son so that, although I might feel as though I'm stuck in the Garden of Gethsemane, there is hope in the Resurrection.

I pray also for others who are caught up in hopelessness, that they may soon experience hope. I also want to unite my prayers with those of Pope Francis, asking that lasting peace may be granted to the Holy Land. Amen.

Pray the Rosary, offering it in petition for a restoration of hope in your life and the lives of the people who concern you. Pray also for peace in the Holy Land.

Stepping Out in Faith

Take some time to think about the questions below. Then answer them as honestly as you can so that your heart can continue to grow more and more peaceful.

- What kind of hopelessness are you facing right now?
- How did it come about? What factors contributed to it?
- What would it take for the hopelessness to be resolved?
- What has prohibited you so far from seeking a resolution?
- What little change can you make right now in your attitude that will help you (them) move toward hopefulness?

Make a concrete resolution to take one step toward peace in your heart today.

Day Five: Basilica of the Holy Sepulchre

The Knots of Grief and Loss

Dear young people, let us entrust ourselves to Jesus, let us give ourselves over to Him, because He never disappoints anyone! Only in Christ crucified and risen can we find salvation and redemption. With Him, evil, suffering, and death do not have the last word, because He gives us hope and life: He has transformed the Cross from being an instrument of hate, defeat, and death to being a sign of love, victory, triumph and life.

—Pope Francis[1]

When a loved one dies, it can feel like the end of the world. One minute they're here, the next minute they're gone, it seems, and we're left behind wondering what to do next. Even if the death was the result of a prolonged illness or serious injury, we're never quite ready when it actually happens. The people we love become a part of us, and when they die, they take a part of us with them. It can leave us feeling empty and alone.

There are other ways we can lose someone, ways that don't involve death but that are just as painful. A physical separation (such as a child leaving home) or end of a relationship can affect us as deeply as a death. Whether an attachment is severed by distance or animosity, or a gradual drifting away, it hurts. We may ignore what's happening in hope that, if we don't acknowledge it, it's not real. But when we finally stop and acknowledge what has happened, we can find ourselves enveloped in the ensuing darkness. We may not know what course of action to take or how to deal with the way we're feeling. Others may not understand because they see our situation from a different perspective.

Any type of loss can spiral us into grief. Grief is a natural response to loss, but it can become all-encompassing and devastating. It separates us from the world and locks us in a vacuum of sorrow. We can become so lost in our grief that we lose our ability to function normally and our sense of reality. Grief can go on for days, months, or even years. Some people seem never to be able to work through their grief.

When we're grieving over loss, we can feel like the Psalmist:

> How long, LORD? Will you utterly forget me?
> How long will you hide your face from me?
> How long must I carry sorrow in my soul,
> grief in my heart day after day?
> How long will my enemy triumph over me?
> Look upon me, answer me, LORD, my God!
> Give light to my eyes lest I sleep in death,
> Lest my enemy say, "I have prevailed,"
> lest my foes rejoice at my downfall. (Ps 13:2–5)

Signs from the Holy Land: At the Tomb

During his time in Jerusalem, Pope Francis's actions spoke far more loudly than his words. I followed with great interest the reports of his activities in this holy city. Of course, his meeting with Ecumenical Patriarch of Constantinople Bartholomew I, spiritual leader of the Eastern Orthodox Church, garnered worldwide attention. The meeting marked the fiftieth anniversary of the meeting between Pope Paul VI and Ecumenical Patriarch of Constantinople Athenagoras. The purpose of both meetings was to further the efforts to reunite the Churches of the East and West.

This is what Pope Paul VI said about his 1964 pilgrimage to the Holy Land:

> There is a spirit which more and more influences Christian hearts. It is the desire to carry out what the Apostle to the Nations counselled us: to forget what is past and push on to what lies ahead, with our eyes fixed upon Jesus, the Author and Finisher of our faith. This spirit has already been manifested in a concrete way in this Holy City, in the efforts being made by all Christians to work in common accord for the reverent care and fitting veneration of that hallowed place where Our Lord, triumphant on the Cross and victorious over the grave, effected the great mission of reconciliation which He had received from His Father. We salute these expressions of Christian charity which already exist, and we express the earnest desire that they may multiply and expand into every area of our common Christian endeavor.[2]

During his trip to the Holy Land, Pope Francis met, first privately and then publicly, with Patriarch Bartholomew. In the private meeting, which took place at Mount Scopus and lasted twice as long as scheduled, the two leaders signed a joint declaration of their desire for unity—a reflection of their longing for both lungs of the Church to function together. For the public meeting, they met in front of the Church of the Holy Sepulchre.

I waited in the conference hall with the rest of the press corps, watching the live broadcast on the monitor. The pope and patriarch stepped toward each other from opposite directions and joined in the center. Before entering the church, they gave each other a warm embrace.

Inside, they participated in a prayer service with members of the Greek Orthodox, Armenian, and Roman Catholic Churches. The service was truly extraordinary because the three communities usually observe a strict separation when praying inside the church. Members of other churches also were present—Coptic, Syriac, Ethiopian, Anglican, and Lutheran clergy.

This historic moment was made all the more poignant by what the two men had done just prior to the prayer service—together, they had visited three of Christianity's most holy places: Golgotha, the Stone of Unction, and Jesus's tomb.[3] They knelt together and prayed together before the Stone of Unction, a red limestone slab traditionally believed to be the stone upon which Jesus' dead body was anointed for burial after the Crucifixion. Without hesitation, the pope knelt, bowed, and reverently kissed the stone. Then, and together with the patriarch, Pope Francis entered the tomb of Christ and immediately knelt and kissed the tomb—no fanfare; no flowery speeches; just humility and reverence.

Finally, Pope Francis and Patriarch Bartholomew approached Golgotha, stepping solemnly and carefully toward the altar that's built over the spot upon which Jesus was crucified. Except for his white zucchetto and cassock, one could have taken the pontiff for any other pilgrim. He was completely oblivious to the dozens of clergy members, security personnel, and photographers that followed him about. His focus was entirely on the place of our Lord's death.

During the prayer service, Pope Francis gave a brief address that, I think, expresses at least a small part of what went through his mind and heart in that holy place:

> Let us receive the special grace of this moment. We pause in reverent silence before this empty tomb in order to rediscover the grandeur of our Christian vocation: we are men and women of resurrection, and not of death. From this place we learn how to live our lives, the trials of our Churches and of the whole world, in the light of Easter morning. Every injury, every one of our pains and sorrows, has been borne on the shoulders of the Good Shepherd who offered himself in sacrifice and thereby opened the way to eternal life. His open wounds are the cleft through which the torrent of his mercy is poured out upon the world. Let us not allow ourselves to be robbed of the basis of our hope![4]

The Church of the Holy Sepulchre is the holiest Christian site in the world and encompasses both Golgotha and the Tomb of the Resurrection. For that reason, the Eastern Orthodox Church refers to it as the Church of the Resurrection. From the earliest times, Christians have held liturgical celebrations there, and in AD 326, Constantine the Great commissioned the first Church of the Holy Sepulchre to be built over the holy sites. Through the centuries, the original structure was destroyed, rebuilt, and renovated to the point that it's now a hodgepodge of architectural styles and constructions.

What struck me hardest was the poverty of it. The custodial communities of the Basilica of the Holy Sepulchre are not rich by any means, and it shows in the church's furnishings. I felt so sad for them, trying so hard to keep up this place of unparalleled holiness; I could see what a struggle it is for them. That instilled in me a sense of mission that continues in my heart to this day—to encourage whoever can to contribute to the collections for the Holy Land and pilgrimage there as soon as possible. I likened it to living far away from your dad's grave. You love your dad, and you honor him, and so you want his grave to be well cared for even if you never get a chance to visit it. The holy places, like the Church of the Holy Sepulchre, are much more than a dad's grave!

Once I got past my shock over the condition of the building, I was able to focus on the holy sites themselves. Actually, focus is a misnomer because I felt utterly unfocused the entire time I was there.

There was so much to take in, and so much going on in my mind and heart, that I actually felt unsteady physically. Not in any way did my prior reading of the scriptures prepare me for this. To stand right at the place where they nailed Jesus to the Cross, to see the notch carved into the peak of Golgotha, to peer at the spot where Mary held her dead son, and then to step inside Jesus' tomb—the place of the Resurrection—was far more than overwhelming.

I was overwrought with grief. Suddenly it seemed as though every sin I had ever committed in my life came rushing at me, and the pain I had caused the Savior because of them was crushing. The realization of the love that it took for Jesus to be able to do that for me nearly crippled me. I was so overwrought, in fact, that I barely wrote anything in the travel journal I'd brought with me. On Golgotha's peak, there's an altar, and under the altar are glass panels that show the rock below. There's a small hole in the glass panel through which you can reach your hand to touch the rock. I almost couldn't bring myself to do it at first. But, gathering my courage, I knelt down, leaned under the altar, and reached through the hole. When I felt the rock below, I lost all sense of time and place. I tried to form a sensible prayer, but couldn't. All I could do was whisper over and over again, "Thank you, thank you, thank you."

On our way to the Tomb of Christ—encased in a small chapel right in the center of the church—we stopped at the Stone of Unction. Oddly, I suddenly became nervous, almost fearful about touching the place where the Lord's body was prepared for burial. I was hesitant to approach it, and stood back a few feet watching the other pilgrims stoop or kneel and then gently kiss or touch the stone.

Finally, I took a pensive step forward, leaned down, laid my hand on the corner of the stone, and then quickly pulled it away. The flood of emotions filling my heart was nearly too much to bear. I felt sorrow, grief, loss, and love like I've never felt before, all welling up inside of me to the point of wanting to throw myself on top of the stone and cry until I could cry no more. It took all my strength to hold it in so as not to cause a scene. I was thinking, here is where his mutilated, crucified body was cleansed and embalmed. His body lay, having borne all of my sins without ever having sinned. The grief I felt then surpassed any grief I've ever known. It was far more than when my dad died when I was just fifteen, and far more than the day we miscarried our second child. It was simply overwhelming.

I wondered how it was on that terrible day for the Blessed Mother and all those who loved Jesus to rest his body on the stone in order to prepare it for burial. As our group walked toward the Educule (tomb of Christ), I pictured Jesus' loved ones carrying his body in and laying it to rest. They, too, must have been overwhelmed by loss and grief. When I peered into the tomb itself, I was reminded that after death comes resurrection—for our Lord, but also for all who follow his ways. Jesus died and rose so that we could die and rise.

Viewing Our Interior Landscape

When we suffer loss, we can feel as though we're standing on the peak of Golgotha, as though—in some strange way—we are both standing at the foot of the Cross and hanging on it ourselves. We can feel as though all of our hopes and dreams have been dashed to the rocks and as though nothing will ever be the same again. The pain is unbearable, the grief immeasurable.

It doesn't matter, really, how old the person was or how the death occurred. Loss is loss, and the pain is a constant; yet it can also be compounded with regret and misgiving, even misplaced guilt, as in the case of a suicide or miscarriage. People who mean well can also do or say things that add to our pain:

- "Cheer up. You can have another baby."
- "He's in a better place, so don't worry."
- "Now you can get on with your life instead of having to care for her."

They don't mean to hurt us, but they do. And whether the loss we experience is from a death or some other tragedy—a financial setback, a scandal, or another devastating blow—we have one we can turn to, even if all our friends and family desert us, or criticize us for not moving on as quickly as they'd like.

Our Lady suffered loss, and she experienced grief. She understands our pain. She walked the *Via Dolorosa* with our Lord, feeling each excruciating blow, flesh-tearing lash, and bone-bruising tumble. When the thorns broke through Jesus' skull, she felt it with him. When the nails pierced his holy hands and feet, she winced and cried out. She stood at the foot of the cross, agonizing with her son, with the weight of all the loss and grief of all of humanity pressing on her heart. She cradled his dead body in her arms. She, of all people, understands loss and grief.

What's more, she understands *our* loss and grief, and cares about our particular devastation. She wants to lighten its weight on our hearts and help us to move through it. She's ready now, this minute, waiting for us to place our knots of loss and grief into her hands so that she can undo them and free us from their pain. Through her compassionate, Immaculate Heart, she intercedes for us and stands ready to undo the knots of pain and grief, so our softened hearts might feel the tender compassion of God and begin to share it with someone else who needs it, too.

The Journey Begins: Let Us Pray for the Gift of Compassion

Our Lady, Undoer of Knots,

I'm sorry for the loss and grief that you had to bear, for the passion you endured as you watched your son stumble toward Calvary. I know that my sinfulness caused your pain, and made it necessary for Our Lord to endure his passion and crucifixion to gain salvation for us all. Thank you, Mother, for enduring such horrible pain for our sake, for my sake.

The loss and grief that I bear right now seems more than I can handle. At times, my pain overwhelms and crushes me. No one else seems to truly understand what I'm going through, and I often feel all alone in my pain. And yet, I know that I am truly not alone, that in your compassion you stay with me, always ready and waiting to share my sorrow.

Help me, please, to believe and feel that you are here, very close to me, accompanying me in my loss and grief. Assure me of your nearness, and help me to surrender this knot of [name the knot] into your willing and capable hands. Show me, step by step, how to let go of the pain and reach for the joy of the Resurrection, and to share your compassion with others who need you as much as I do. Mother, with you, I want not to

> wallow in the sorrow of the Cross, but rather to proclaim its victory.
>
> I pray also for others who are weighted down with loss and grief, that they may soon feel secure in Jesus' and your love for them. I also want to unite my prayers with those of Pope Francis, asking that lasting peace may be granted to the Holy Land. Amen.

Pray the Rosary, offering it in petition for the relief of your grief and for those who grieve with you. Pray also for peace in the Holy Land.

Stepping Out in Faith

Take some time to think about the questions below. Then answer them as honestly as you can so that your heart can continue to grow more and more peaceful.

- What loss have you experienced?
- What is it about this loss that hurts the most?
- Does this loss elicit fears in you? What are they?
- Where can you see God's guiding hand in the circumstances of this loss?
- The loss cannot be replaced, but can you think of anything that will help you start to feel "normal" again? What is it?

Make a concrete resolution to take one step toward peace in your heart today.

Day Six: Western Wall

The Knot of Discord

Discord among Christians is the greatest obstacle to evangelization. It fosters the growth of groups that take advantage of people's poverty and credulity to propose easy but illusory solutions to their problems. In a world wounded by so many ethnic, political, and religious conflicts, communities must become "authentically fraternal and reconciled" so that in them "they will find that witness luminous and attractive." God gives us the grace, if we

> know how to receive it, to make unity prevail over conflict.
>
> —Pope Francis[1]

Discord is all around us. We can see it on both a national level (such as the 2014 riots following the Michael Brown shooting in Ferguson, Missouri), as well as on a global level (such as the ongoing conflicts in the Middle East). Discord can also affect us locally, creating conflict in our communities and parishes and turning people against each other. Many of us face discord in our own families, perhaps in our own homes and even in our hearts.

Discord can happen between individuals, groups, cultures, religions, or nations. Often, it begins with something very small—a minor detail that gets blown out of proportion and becomes a major point of contention. It can begin with misunderstanding and lack of communication. In many cases, it is rooted in long-standing prejudices and fears. No matter the cause, discord's intensity grows exponentially and can leave both emotional and physical destruction in its wake.

The root of discord can be egoism, pride, greed, desire for power, or simple stubbornness. It could also be a combination of any or all of those. It can even stem from ignorance. Discord happens when people, for whatever reason, fail to meet in the middle or to see things from the perspective of the other. They believe that they are right and that what they're doing is somehow deserved and just. When someone—or many people, for that matter—are convinced that they are blameless or not fully to blame, they are unmotivated to seek resolution or reconciliation in order to achieve or restore peaceful communion.

Signs from the Holy Land: Waiting and Wailing

The Wailing Wall (or Western Wall), a remnant of a retaining wall from the Second Temple, is the holiest of Jewish sites and one of the most pronounced symbols of discord in the Holy Land. Jews go there to pray and lament the horrors inflicted upon their people by the Romans and subsequent loss of the Temple.

On the last morning of his three-day pilgrimage to the Holy Land, Pope Francis met with Muslims and Jews and called for an end to the discord in the region. He visited the Dome of the Rock on the Temple Mount, a sacred place for Muslims because tradition holds that this is where Mohammed had a vision of heaven.

The Holy Father spoke to Muslims, Jews, and Christians alike, calling them "brothers" rather than "friends," as was written in his prepared text. He pointed to Abraham—who left his home and his people in order to follow God's call—as a model for Muslims, Jews, and Christians.

"We must constantly be prepared to go out from ourselves, docile to God's call, especially his summons to work for peace and justice, to implore these gifts in prayer and to learn from on high mercy, magnanimity and compassion," the pope said.[2]

After the meeting, Pope Francis proceeded to the Western Wall, approaching the wall slowly and reverently, and once there, carefully placed his right hand against the wall. He bowed his head in silent prayer and remained there for a minute and a half. Then he thoughtfully recited the Our Father and, following custom, he deposited a folded piece of paper into a crack in the wall. Pilgrims write prayers on the papers; the Holy Father's paper contained the Our Father written in Spanish. Later, he explained that he'd written it in Spanish because that's the language he learned from his mother.

Sensitivity—this was the word that came to mind as I watched the reports of the pope's visit to the Western Wall. I know this word is misused and overused in modern society. Usually, it's used in efforts to be politically correct and in regard to minority groups. But that's not the kind of sensitivity I mean. Rather, he seemed to have all of his senses at peak, taking everything in with the utmost care and to the utmost degree. Additionally, I mean his mental, spiritual, and emotional sensitivities. He seemed keenly aware of the religious importance of the place, and he felt it deeply in his heart. He also knew the historical significance, and the suffering that it represented. He felt the anguish of the Jewish people over their loss. With his body language and the few words he did speak, Pope Francis sent a message of sensitivity and appreciation to the whole world.

When I saw the Western Wall for myself, I was struck by the enormity of it. In my mind's eye, I'd pictured it as about twice the height of a tall man. It's much more than that! Leading up to the wall is the Western Wall Plaza, a paved open space that accommodates tens of thousands of worshippers. The wall itself is 105 feet from its underground foundation to its highest point; approximately fifteen feet deep and 1,600 feet long. Not only is the Western Wall the only remnant of the Temple, but it's also the wall that is believed to have been the closest to the Holy of Holies. The wall consists of layers of large stones—the lowest ones having been cut and fitted by Herod's masons. On top of the Herodian stones are layers from various time periods, but the ones of Herod's time are distinguishable by their chiseled edges and outstanding craftsmanship, given the tools available during that period. They range from 2.5 to 44.6 feet in length and 3.6 to 11.5 feet in height. Even without taking into account the wall's religious purpose, it's a majestic structure in and of itself.[3]

As much as the structure itself stunned me, the people and their customs stunned me even more. When we entered the plaza, men and women were separated—men went to one side of the long, person-high screen that made a line down the center, and women to the other. Men must wear a hat or take a free head covering from a box beside the entrance to the prayer area. Women, who must also be modestly attired, may borrow shawls and short skirt coverings before entering their side of the screen.

The next thing I observed were people walking backward away from the wall. Our guide must have noticed the look of curiosity on my face, because she leaned over and whispered, "You're not supposed to ever turn your back to the wall." Sure enough, every person who walked toward the wall walked away from it backward. Even those standing or sitting on the plaza kept their faces to it.

My next surprise was the sound and movement of the worshippers. I'd never seen Jewish prayer before, and so I had no idea that they pray in motion and with spontaneous vocalization. They sway, rock, spin, and raise their hands to heaven; they wail, moan, recite, and cry out. Suddenly, a man on the other side of the screen began shrieking—a blood-curdling shriek—and I froze. Again, our guide rescued me. "He's okay. That's the way they pray," she assured me. I must have seemed in disbelief, because she leaned over again and said, "He's okay. Really. I promise." I took a deep breath and continued on toward the wall.

At first glimpse, it can be disconcerting to someone unfamiliar with Jewish prayer customs. But when

I put my preconceived notions of "proper" prayer aside, I actually found myself in awe and then admiration. How incredible that they can be so uninhibited in prayer! Nothing hinders them from completely and comprehensively expressing themselves to God. I thought of how subdued my own prayer is in comparison, and wondered what it would be like to be so engrossed that I could pray without inhibition as the people around me were that day.

As I stood there, taking all of this in, it dawned on me that this place was not only holy because it was a Jewish temple, but because it was *the* Jewish Temple. This exact same Temple was where Joseph and Mary presented the infant Jesus and where Mary received purification. Here is where Simeon recognized the Savior and foretold of the sword that would pierce Mary's heart. Here the prophetess Anna proclaimed the Redeemer. To this Temple, our Lord traveled annually with his parents. Here is where Joseph and Mary found the young Jesus after three days of panicked searching. Jesus chased the money changers out of this Temple and taught here many times. It was to this Temple that he rode on a donkey from the Mount of Olives on Palm Sunday and over which he wept. Behind the Temple was the fortress that Herod had built in 35 BC, called Antonia. It's believed Jesus was taken there to be condemned by Pontius Pilate and was quite possibly where the scourging took place. It was here, also, that Paul was arrested by the Roman soldiers, addressed the hostile crowd, and was imprisoned for his own protection. This place wasn't only a vital part of Jewish heritage; it was a part of *my* heritage.

The discord that had affected the Jewish people for centuries affected me, too. The discord between the Romans and the Jews, between Muslims, Christians, and Jews, and between the Sadducees and Pharisees and our Lord and his disciples had left its impression on the stones of the Western Wall, and I felt the misery.

Viewing Our Interior Landscape

That's what discord does to us: it leaves us in misery. It becomes a knot that holds us fast—neither able to move backward nor forward. It's as if the knot that's holding us is suspended in time and space. We try not to think of it, but it's forever present in our minds and hearts.

After a falling out with someone close to us (or even an acquaintance we frequently encounter in the workplace, school, or parish), it can be easy to become stuck in the resolve to "make" the other person reach out first. In other cases, when we are indirectly involved in the conflict, it can be easy to become caught between the two "sides." How stressful it can be to overcome these relational walls, and restore interpersonal communion!

Our Lady knows what it's like to be encompassed in discord. She lived all her life as a Jew among Roman occupation and persecution. She must have witnessed the many conflicts between the Zealots and Herod's soldiers. She saw her people endure their oppressive domination. She received the prophecy of Simeon that foretold great suffering ahead for her son and herself. Jesus, he said, would be "destined for the fall and rise of many in Israel and to be a sign that will be contradicted" (Lk 2:34). Contraction can be another word for discord, and it was part of Mary's destiny.

Because Mary withstood discord herself, she understands what it's like for us to withstand and endure in such circumstances. And because she's our wise and attentive Mother, she understands us and how the discord is affecting us. She longs to draw us close—to herself and to one another—out of her love for us. She wants us to open ourselves to the possibility of communion restored.

The Journey Begins: Let Us Pray for Sincere Humility

Our Lady, Undoer of Knots,

You understand discord because you witnessed it in your lifetime on earth. You've seen what happens when people are at odds and you see the sinfulness of their folly. Discord was part of the sword that pierced your Immaculate Heart and the reason your Son became a sign of contradiction.

Mother, you understand my discord because you know all about me—what affects me and what I have to endure. You know how this discord came to be, and you know what must happen for it to end. You know, also, any responsibility I might bear for its cause or continuation, and yet you love me still. And you know all about the others involved, and you love them still, too.

Please accept this knot of discord [name the knot]. Take it into your skillful hands and untie it, one snarl at a time, so that the ribbon of my life can be free of discord and its consequences. Help me to remain strong as you work on it, because the resolution of discord can often require great courage and fortitude. If I am at fault, show me how and then show me what to do to make amends. Make me truly desire the knot to be undone so that I can follow your guidance with a sincere heart and put forth genuine effort on my part.

Dear Lady, pray for me and all those bound by this knot. I pray for them, too, and for all those caught in knots of discord throughout the world, particularly in areas of conflict and strife. I also want to unite my prayers with those of Pope Francis, asking that lasting peace may be granted to the Holy Land. Amen.

Pray the Rosary, offering it in petition for the resolution of the discord you're experiencing and for those involved with you. Pray also for peace in the Holy Land.

Stepping Out in Faith

Take some time to think about the questions below. Then answer them as honestly as you can so that your heart can continue to grow more and more peaceful.

- How did this discord begin? What caused it?
- Regardless of who seems to be at fault, what part did you play in the tying of this knot?
- What do you think made the other(s) involved act that way?
- What made you act that way?
- What can be done differently from now on to help ease, if not end, the discord?

Make a concrete resolution to take one step toward peace in your heart today.

Day Seven:
Yad Vashem, Mount of Remembrance

The Knot of Betrayal

> Think carefully about this: God comes to live with men, he chooses the earth as his dwelling in order to stay . . . where man passes his days in joy or in sorrow. Therefore the earth is above all not a "valley of tears" but a place where God himself has pitched his tent. It is the place of meeting for God with man, of solidarity of God with men.
>
> —Pope Francis[1]

Betrayal can be devastating and highly destructive to both our relationships and reputation. We seldom expect it, and rarely know what to do about it. Once that trust has been broken, restoring it can be difficult, even impossible. (At times it is also inadvisable, if the person who betrayed us did so knowingly and maliciously.)

Generally, when we think about betrayal, we associate it with Judas Iscariot. Jesus himself referred to Judas as a betrayer. "Get up, let us go. Look, my betrayer is at hand," he told his disciples in the Garden of Gethsemane (Mt 26:46). Then Judas betrayed our Lord with a kiss, handing him over to the chief priests for execution. No one can be certain whether or not Judas knew Jesus would be crucified once he'd betrayed him, but he must have been aware that the Pharisees wanted to kill him. It's even possible that he fully expected Jesus would save himself from cruel fate because he was the Messiah, and then was horrified when Jesus meekly accepted condemnation and death. Either way, he was playing a dangerous game with Jesus' life. When he found out about Jesus' sentence, his remorse was so extreme that he committed suicide. Betrayal can twist and turn, becoming a knot that entangles in unforeseen ways.

Betrayal shakes us because it makes us realize that the person who betrayed us isn't the person we thought he or she was; someone we counted on is no longer dependable. It can also affect the way we feel about ourselves. We reproach ourselves, as though we should have known better than to trust, or berate ourselves for not being more aware. We might feel stupid for not "getting it" sooner, or for not knowing how to properly handle the situation. Betrayal can leave us in a jumble of raw nerves and broken heartedness that can take years and years to overcome.

Betrayal occurs, not just between individuals, but also among groups, cultures, and nations. Family feuds aren't just something we see on TV; they are real and destructive as entire branches of families can turn from each other. Within a country, civil war causes groups from different cultures or ethnicities to clash, turning former neighbors into mortal enemies. When the leaders of countries say or do things to show they are no longer trustworthy, this betrayal can destroy thousands of lives in wartime.

Whether on a smaller scale or a broad one, betrayal twists us in a bitter, doleful knot that can color our view of the world. The long-term damage of such betrayal can, in the process, affect multiple aspects of our lives—our work, our relationships, even our future. And so, for our own peace of mind, we must guard against bitterness and vengeful impulses by cultivating the gift of understanding, of seeing the brokenness and bondage of the person who inflicted such wounds upon us. If we are able to do this, the force of the betrayal may be transformed by love, healing all concerned.

Signs from the Holy Land: The Eternal Flame of Recollection

Following in the footsteps of his predecessor, Pope Francis visited Yad Vashem not long after he had visited the Western Wall. In order that the Holocaust might never be forgotten, Yad Vashem—a complex of museums, memorials, and learning centers—was built in Jerusalem and established in 1953. It's become the world's center for documentation, research, education, and commemoration of the Holocaust.

During an official memorial service in the Hall of Remembrance, the pope listened to a choir of Jewish children, rekindled the Eternal Flame, and laid a wreath over the crypt that holds the ashes of the Holocaust victims who were cremated in the extermination camps. The Holy Father's somber address fit his somber surroundings. Since then, his powerful words have been quoted time and again:

> Grant us the grace to be ashamed of what men have done, to be ashamed of this massive idolatry, of having despised and destroyed our own flesh which you formed from the earth, to which you gave life with your own breath of life. Never again, Lord, never again![2]

The Nazi treatment of the Jewish people represented betrayal on a massive scale. Polish Jews were singled out and forced into barren, severely overcrowded, undersupplied, and unsanitary ghettos, which the Nazis tried to mask by calling them "Jewish residential quarters." In effect, they were starved to death. More than two million Polish Jews came under Nazi control, and soon thousands of German and Austrian Jews also were forced into ghettos in Eastern Europe.

Then things got worse as the Nazis implemented a sinister plan to eliminate the entire Jewish race, the "Final Solution," a plan that had been brewing for more than a decade. German death squads, or "special duty units," began murdering entire Jewish communities, either by shooting them en masse or gassing them in vans outfitted especially for that purpose. But this method was inefficient, so the Nazis built six extermination camps in Polish territory: Chelmno, Belzec, Sobibór, Treblinka, Auschwitz-Birkenau, and Majdanek. Additionally, they built eighteen concentration camps, which were either holding centers or forced labor camps.

Death, degradation, starvation, and disease were everywhere, from the ghettos to the work camps. About three million Jews were gassed, and additional atrocities led to the deaths of about six million Jews in all—two thirds of the European Jewish population.

The Jews suffered betrayal on a massive scale.

By the time my group visited Yad Vashem, we'd had a chance to read the transcript of the pope's address. His words "never again, Lord never again" echoed in our heads. I was excited about seeing the

Holocaust Museum, not in a morbid way but in an urgently interested way. One camp in particular had a deep and personal significance for me.

When I was just a year old, I was blessed and consecrated to the Blessed Mother by a holy priest named Fr. Joseph Kentenich (1885–1968), who is the founder of the Apostolic Movement of Schoenstatt, a Catholic lay ecclesial movement and the center of my life since my youth. Fr. Kentenich was visiting the home of our neighbor, and she invited my mother to come meet him. Because I was the only child home at the time, my mother brought me along.

Fr. Kentenich exchanged words with Mom, and then, holding me in his arms, he approached the family's prayer corner. There he lifted me up in front of the picture of Mary, prayed, and then handed me back to my mother. Before parting, Fr. Kentenich presented Mom with the picture of Mary titled, *Mother Thrice Admirable, Queen and Victress of Schoenstatt*. This image is enthroned in the more than two hundred Schoenstatt Marian Shrines around the world and cherished by the movement's members. I'm convinced that Fr. Kentenich's blessing and act of consecrating me to the Blessed Mother has protected me my entire life, even in times of great physical and spiritual danger.

Fr. Kentenich had experienced these protective graces himself under the direst imaginable circumstances, when he was interned by the Nazis at Dachau (1941–45). After being imprisoned by the Gestapo for a year, including a month of solitary confinement in a concrete bunker (a converted bank vault) too small for him to stand upright, Fr. Kentenich was interned with a number of Schoenstatt priests on Block 13, the "priest's block," where 2,579 priests and many seminarians and lay brothers were interned. Starved, degraded, and exposed to extreme elements, these brave men endured sickness and disease, beatings, overwork, and overcrowding. Some of them underwent medical experimentation. More than one thousand priests died in Dachau.[3]

In the midst of this, Fr. Kentenich gave of himself untiringly, holding talks and retreats, hearing confessions, and giving spiritual counsel to the other prisoners. All was done secretly under the guards' watch, while working, walking the grounds, or standing (sometimes for hours) at roll call. Fr. Kentenich rose earlier than required for prayer, and shared his meager rations with those who were worse off than he was. While in prison, Fr. Kentenich composed an entire book of prayers titled, *Heavenwards,* which has become the "bible" of the Schoenstatt Movement.

Although it hasn't been medically proven, anecdotal evidence suggests and Fr. Kentenich himself later testified that he came out of the camp more physically fit than he went in. Given the conditions, this can only be attributed to God's grace. Other prisoners have testified to Fr. Kentenich's holy example while in Dachau. His process for canonization is ongoing in

Rome, and he's been given the title Servant of God by the Holy See.

Knowing all of this has made Dachau important to me. I've never visited there in person, and so I was eager to experience what I could of it at Yad Vashem.

Our docent, Zellie, was introduced to us as the "very best" of their guides, and she was very good at her job. She was both personable and knowledgeable; I liked her right away. Zellie first took us through the Hall of Names, a cylinder-shaped memorial that contains row after row of binders on shelves going far below and far above the visitors' platform. Each page contained the name and personal information of a Holocaust victim. The Hall of Names has room for six million of the victims' pages, and the research institute has recovered the names and information of 4.3 million so far. The project will continue until they have all been recovered.

I've read in history books about the vast number of Jews who were killed by Hitler's henchmen, but until I saw the Hall of Names, it was just a number in a chapter or an article. Standing on that platform, and looking around and around at volume after volume after volume—all filled with pages of names representing real people who lived and loved—put a lump in my throat and left me awestruck. The Hall also contains thousands and thousands of pictures of the Holocaust victims, and looking at them brought tears to my eyes. One in particular strikingly resembled my mother's high school graduation picture, and I wondered to myself if that was the high school graduation picture of someone else's mom.

We finally got to the museum, and Zellie led us through, beginning with exhibits portraying the rise of the Nazi regime and progressing through the implementation of the Final Solution. Among the exhibits was a section on the Catholic Church's part in the Holocaust, which I found disconcerting. It seemed to me that the anti-Semitic actions (or indifference) of a small minority of Catholics was being applied to the whole Church, something that is demonstrably unjust.

Although some Catholics did resent the Jews or turn a blind eye to the Holocaust, not all of them did. Pope Piux XII himself worked heroically to save a documented 700,000 to 860,000 Jews from extermination.[4] Catholic men and women, including clergy and religious, worked tirelessly to resist the Nazis—and many wound up dying in the camps themselves. By the end of Hitler's reign, millions of Catholics had died on the battlefield, under forced labor, or as victims in the gas chambers. Catholic churches, monasteries, convents, schools, and monuments had been destroyed.

And so, when Zellie turned to us and declared, "Yes, all of this and the Church did nothing. Absolutely nothing!" I knew she was wrong. And yet, I also understood the sense of betrayal that gave rise to her words. Since much of her family had died in the Holocaust, she had reason to feel betrayed. If she was unaware of the documented actions of Catholics on behalf of the Jewish people, I could see how she might have felt betrayed by the Church, too. I prayed for an opportunity to share what I knew.

Zellie continued our tour, pointing out artifacts from the various camps, each one with its own section. On large screens stationed throughout, documentary-style movies played, giving further explanation. We went from one to the other—Auschwitz, Majdanek, Treblinka, Chelmno, and others. It was tragic and it put a pall of sorrow over me. As we neared the end of the camp sections, however, I still hadn't seen anything about Dachau. So, I waited for a pause in her presentation, and then approached Zellie.

"Zellie, where is Dachau?" I asked.

She turned to me, with a look of astonishment. "Dachau? Dachau? Dachau was nothing!" she said. "There were just some political prisoners there."

Because of my personal connection to the place where Fr. Kentenich was imprisoned, that pretty much burned my fuse to its end. "Zellie, did you know that more than two thousand Catholic priests were imprisoned in Dachau?" I asked her.

I didn't know how to interpret the blank look she gave me, but at that moment, I needed to say what was on my mind. I explained that the priests in Dachau were starved, beaten, made to stand hours on end in even the most severe weather, and made to work beyond the capacity of human strength and on very little sleep. Many died of starvation, disease, and medical·experimentation.

"Zellie, I know one of those priests," I concluded. "He blessed me when I was a baby. I know how he suffered."

Her eyebrows shot up in her jaw dropped. "I had no idea!" She exclaimed.

"Dachau is very important to me," I said as gently as I could. "It was more than just holding place for political prisoners."

Zellie got very quiet for a minute, and then continued the tour. She next took us to the Children's Memorial, an underground cavern that is darkened and solemn. As visitors walk through the passageway, small lights flicker, representing the 1.5 million Jewish children killed during the Holocaust. A voice speaks the name, age, and country of origin of each of the children. I thought about how painful it was to miscarry our second child, and was sorrowful for the parents of these children. But then I realized that they had probably died in Holocaust, too. And I wept.

The final stop in our tour was the Hall of Remembrance. We saw the wreath that Pope Francis had placed there the day before, and the Eternal Flame that burns forever in honor of the Holocaust victims. The floor holds twenty-two concrete tiles. On each is engraved the name of one of the most infamous Nazi murder sites, symbolizing the hundreds of the Nazi extermination and concentration camps.

As I stood at the railing looking over the tiles, Zellie came up beside me and put her arm around my shoulder. She leaned over and pointed. "There is Dachau," she said, indicating a tile just to our right. Then, she gave my shoulder a little squeeze and rounded up the tour.

Viewing Our Interior Landscape

My encounter with Zellie that day reminded me that people are not always conscious of the ways in which betrayal colors our view of the world. We can become so used to harboring bitterness and sorrow in our hearts that it starts to feel completely normal to us. If the bitterness goes too deep and our view becomes too colored, it even can lead us to betraying someone else, creating a bigger and bigger tangle of knots.

Have you been betrayed, or perhaps even betrayed someone else? Perhaps a friend shared something you'd spoken in confidence. Maybe you found yourself the subject of lies and gossip from prying relatives. A coworker might have used deception to rob you of an advancement you deserved. Maybe your spouse has committed adultery. Any of these scenarios can be absolutely soul crushing. Committing these sins against another person creates an inner burden or knot of an entirely different kind; Our Lady is waiting to receive them all.

And so, this is the perfect time to turn to Our Lady, Undoer of Knots. She understands betrayal—her son was betrayed by one of his closest followers, and she accompanied him through his passion and crucifixion. Because she loved Jesus so much, his betrayal was her betrayal, too. She knew the apostles, and she felt the pain of Judas's treachery. She experienced the devastation as she stood at the foot of the cross. She listened to Peter's heartbroken outburst, as he confessed to his risen Lord the threefold denial that had become his deepest, darkest regret.

Our Lady, Undoer of Knots, understands your betrayal because she knows your story and what lies in your heart. Just as she accompanied Jesus through his suffering, she accompanies you through yours. She wants to ease your pain, and she is eagerly waiting to unravel the knot of betrayal in your life. In order to do that, she needs you to let go of the knot so that she can take it up in her hands.

The Journey Begins: Let Us Pray

Our Lady, Undoer of Knots,

You know that I'm trapped in this knot of betrayal. Please help me. You know how I became trapped, and you know how to get me out. You know the effects it has had on me and what it will take for me to heal.

Mother, please touch my heart and begin the healing process right now. Ease the pain, and calm my mind and heart from the bitterness and sorrow that I bear. Help me not to hate and resent, but rather to forgive and let go.

I place this knot of betrayal into your hands, knowing that you have the ability to unwind the snarls and untie it. Help me to trust you completely, even though I'm finding it difficult to trust others. Remind me of the betrayal your son endured so that he will be my example of suffering in humility.

I also place into your hands those who have betrayed me. Take them into your hands, into your heart, and help them to understand the difficulty they've caused and the damage that has resulted. Please help them to have a change of heart and mind open to the truth.

Our Lady, Undoer of Knots, pray for me and for my betrayer(s). I pray for them, also, and for all those who are ensnared in the knot of betrayal. I also want to unite my prayers with those of Pope Francis, asking that lasting peace may be granted to the Holy Land. Amen.

Pray the Rosary, offering it in petition for those who have betrayed you, and those who you have betrayed, either intentionally or unintentionally. Ask for mutual forgiveness and healing for all involved. Pray also for peace in the Holy Land.

Stepping Out in Faith

Take some time to think about the questions below. Then answer them as honestly as you can so that your heart can continue to grow more and more peaceful.

- What were the circumstances of your betrayal?
- How has it made you feel?
- Why do you think you feel that way? (Be honest with yourself.)
- How has your view of the world been colored because of this?
- Can you forgive your betrayer? If not, can you bring yourself to pray for the desire to forgive? How might you do that?

Make a concrete resolution to take one step toward peace in your heart today.

Day Eight:

Temple Mount

The Knots of Envy and Pride

What is the law of the People of God? It is the law of love, love for God and love for neighbor according to the new commandment that the Lord left to us (cf. Jn 13:34). It is a love, however, that is not sterile sentimentality or something vague, but the acknowledgment of God as the one Lord of life and, at the same time, the acceptance of the other as my true brother, overcoming division, rivalry, misunderstanding, selfishness; these two things go together. . . .We must ask the Lord to make us correctly understand this law of love. How beautiful it is

to love one another as true brothers and sisters.
How beautiful! Let's do something today.

—Pope Francis[1]

When you were in high school, did you ever find yourself feeling resentful of the most popular kids in your class? Did you roll your eyes behind their backs and to their faces pretend that you didn't care? Privately, you probably wished that you could be like them. Is it possible that you were envious of their popularity?

Or, perhaps you were one of the popular ones, enjoying all of the attention and accolade that went with it. You cherished your privileged station in the class and maybe sometimes you even flaunted it. You might have felt as though you deserved it and treated the other kids accordingly. Is it possible that you were prideful of your popularity? Or did you secretly envy some of your less-popular classmates because they had something you did not—top grades, attentive parents, or the right prom date?

Most of us have had experiences like that at one time or another in our lives. It's easy to be envious of others, especially when there is an apparent inequality in possessions, attributes, or honor. Just think of the number of times you've driven past a really expensive, well-maintained house and dreamed about being its owner. We can succumb to pride without even realizing it, like when we gloat about having something that others don't or when we're too proud to ask for help. Just think of the age-old arguments between men and women about asking for directions when lost. We don't like to ask directions because we'd be admitting that we don't know everything.

Envy and pride are as easy to fall into as they are dangerous. They're so dangerous, in fact, that they are two of what the Church refers to as the seven capital sins. These sins are so-called because they engender other sins and vices. The five other capital sins are avarice, wrath, lust, gluttony, and sloth or acedia (CCC 1866).

Envy is prohibited by the tenth commandment and is defined in the *Catechism* as "the sadness at the sight of another's goods and the immoderate desire to acquire them for oneself, even unjustly" (CCC 2539). When envy becomes so strong that it makes us wish harm to the person we envy, it becomes a mortal sin.

The prophet Nathan helped King David understand envy by telling him a story about a poor man who had only one ewe lamb and treated it like his own daughter. There was a rich man who, despite his large flock, envied the poor man and ended up stealing his lamb. Envy can lead to other sins. In fact, St. John Chrysostom said in one of his homilies that, through the devil's envy, death entered the world.[2] St. Augustine taught that envy gives way to hatred, detraction, calumny, joy over another's misfortune, and displeasure at his prosperity. It's refusal of charity and often comes from pride (CCC 2540).

Pride violates the first commandment and can be defined as a self-love that seeks attention and honor to the point of setting oneself in competition with God. Prideful people might consider themselves better than they really are, and take personal credit for gifts or possessions without acknowledging God's goodness. Prideful people minimize their own defects and take glory in their own achievements, even if it wasn't solely a result of their efforts. They might hold themselves superior and even disdain others because they lack something the prideful person has.

Pride can become so severe that it leads to hatred of God. "It is contrary to love of God, whose goodness it denies, and whom it presumes to curse as the one who forbids sins and inflicts punishments," the *Catechism* states (CCC 2094).

None of us likes to be envious of someone else, but we often are. Usually, we don't like it when others are envious of us either. None of us truly likes to be prideful, but we often are. And most of us have a really hard time dealing with others who are prideful.

Envy and pride contrive knots that bind us to our own sinfulness and separate us from others. They can even separate us from God, a tiny seed of resentment that can grow into an insurmountable chasm of hatred. Each of these tiny seeds must be recognized, weeded out, and replaced with the gentle virtues of humility and contentment.

Signs from the Holy Land: A View from the Other Side

On the early morning of May 26, Pope Francis met with the Grand Mufti of Jerusalem. The Mufti accompanied the pope as he visited Temple Mount, and they were accompanied by a group of Muslim and Catholic clerics. The Holy Father removed his shoes before entering the Dome of the Rock, which is the third holiest place in Islam, where Muslims believe Mohammed ascended to heaven. It's a holy place for Jews as well because it's where the First Temple and Second Temple were destroyed. Christians honor the site because it is believed that this is where the sacrifice of Isaac took place. Rich with holy symbolism, Temple Mount is one of the most highly contested sites in the Muslim-Jewish division.

Pope Francis clearly had it in mind to urge the religious leaders associated with the Mount toward a peaceful cooperation. Muslim media later reported that during the pope's private meeting with the Grand Mufti, he pleaded with him to disavow violence and find a way to work together with the Jews in maintaining this holy place.[3]

Two paragraphs from Pope Francis's discourse to the Grand Mufti particularly impress me. The first one is this:

> A pilgrim is a person who makes himself poor and sets forth on a journey. Pilgrims set out intently

> toward a great and longed-for destination, and they live in the hope of a promise received (cf. Heb 11:8–19). This was how Abraham lived, and this should be our spiritual attitude. We can never think ourselves self-sufficient, masters of our own lives. We cannot be content with remaining withdrawn, secure in our convictions. Before the mystery of God we are all poor. We realize that we must constantly be prepared to go out from ourselves, docile to God's call and open to the future that he wishes to create for us.[4]

These words of the Holy Father seem to me to be the perfect prescription for avoiding envy and pride. He was addressing two groups of people who have been allowing their envy and pride to become so intense that it's led to open conflict on Temple Mount and elsewhere. When we believe that we are masters of our own lives, rather than God, we'll be conflicted and unable to have peace in our hearts, in our families, and in the world around us.

The second paragraph from the pope's discourse that impressed me is this:

> Nor can we forget that the pilgrimage of Abraham was also a summons to righteousness: God wanted him to witness his way of acting and to imitate him. We too wish to witness to God's working in the world, and so, precisely in this

> meeting, we hear deep within us his summons to work for peace and justice, to implore these gifts in prayer and to learn from on high mercy, magnanimity and compassion.[5]

Mercy, magnanimity, and compassion are antidotes for the poison of envy and pride.

My group spent a full day in Jerusalem, visiting the holy sites and getting to know the city. On many of our stops, we could see Temple Mount in all its glory. It really is beautiful to look at, with its golden dome that glistens in the pure Israeli sunshine.

At one point, we went to the Austrian Hospice of the Holy Family, a 150-year-old facility that's known for the astounding view from its roof terrace. It's right in the heart of the Old City of Jerusalem and directly on the *Via Dolorosa*, or the traditional pilgrim path of the Stations of the Cross. From the terrace, we could see most of the landmarks and holy sites of Jerusalem. The panoramic view is simply breathtaking!

The building itself was a marvel. I was so busy taking in the ambience and historical significance of the place that I forgot to watch my step and nearly stumbled going up some steps. It's built in the style of a palace on Vienna's *Ringstrasse*, a circular drive in Vienna that's admired for its architectural, historical, and scenic qualities. In its day, it really was hospice for travelers and residents of Jerusalem. Today, it's a guest house and intercultural center.[6]

Our guide pointed out the various sites, and then we took some time to rest in the quiet and loveliness of this little oasis high above the Jerusalem streets. From our vantage point, Temple Mount stood out among all the other structures. Until my trip to Israel, I had no idea that the Dome of the Rock had any Jewish or Christian significance. I had assumed that it was strictly a Muslim site. I thought about what the mount means to the Jews—and by association, what it meant to our Lord, Mary, and Joseph. They, too, mourned the destruction of the Temples, and they also had cherished the story of Abraham and Isaac. Temple Mount was important to the Holy Family.

As I stood there, with the warm, late-afternoon breeze blowing over me, I was filled with emotions that were strange and hard to describe. It was almost as if I was experiencing a conflict of my own in a small way. There was the dome, which was important to all three religions—Muslim, Jewish, and Christian. All three are very different in their beliefs, and yet at the same time all three hold Temple Mount equally in esteem and reverence. Yet, over the centuries and until today, places such as Temple Mount were the scenes of brutal battles between them. How could that possibly be?

I think that at that moment, more than any other while I was in Israel, I was struck by the magnitude of the causes and consequences of conflict in the Middle East. I was surprised many times during our trip by the realization that so many of the sites I saw through my Catholic lens, other religions were looking at through their lenses. It was mind-boggling for me.

I looked at Temple Mount, and then I looked across the city. Jerusalem is divided into four quarters, or neighborhoods, that are named after the ethnic groups that live in them: Christian, Jewish, Muslim, and Armenian. It seemed so ironic that all of these people live in their own separate quarters, and yet they appreciate some of the same holy sites. Temple Mount seemed like a beacon shining high above the city, reminding me of this irony.

Viewing Our Interior Landscape

Envy and pride can lead us to segregate our lives into quarters, like the Old City of Jerusalem, in the sense that we separate the "haves" from the "have-nots." Whether it's property, popularity, talents, intelligence, or something entirely different, we can be prideful when we have more than others and envious of those who have more than we do. And yet, ironically, we're all looking to the same "Temple Mount" of holiness and peace. And the way to get there is through the intentional practice of generous mercy.

Perhaps you've had a long-standing, work-related grudge against a company or person. Or you secretly resent a friend who always seems perfectly put together and abundantly talented. Maybe the very sight of a particular loved one brings back feelings of resentment or embarrassment because of something that happened between you that you are unable to forgive or forget. Pride can keep us from letting go of these things.

You might even be envious of suffering. Does it seem as though your suffering is far worse than someone else's? Or, maybe it's the way they're handling their suffering that upsets you; they seem to be managing their suffering with ease while you struggle terribly with yours. That's not only envy, but it's also a form of pride. It's like thinking that you know better than God what suffering is good for you. While it's human nature to compare sufferings and situations, it's dangerous to think that you are better off or worse off than someone else.

These are the times that we need our Mother Mary to help us undo these terrible knots of envy and pride. She is Our Lady, Undoer of Knots, and there is no knot that cannot be undone when placed into her hands. The most severe envy can be turned into charity, and the most stubborn pride can be turned into humility. She has seen the effects of envy and pride in her own time and throughout the centuries, and she assists her son in saving souls by working to untie the knots that get in the way of us recognizing our need to come to her son for salvation.

The Journey Begins: Let Us Pray for Genuine Mercy

Our Lady, Undoer of Knots,

You never once felt envy or pride, yet you suffered the consequences of the envy and pride of other people. You have continued to suffer from the envy and pride of people throughout the centuries because it leads to sin, and sin causes the wounds of your son to be more painful. And when your son is in pain, you also are in pain.

Mother, you see the knots of envy and pride that tangle me in this sinfulness. I'm too weak to untie this knot on my own; I need your help. Please take these knots from me and untie them so that I can be free from envy and pride and all of their effects and consequences.

So, too, I place into your hands all of the people that I envy or who envy me, and all those who are affected by my pridefulness. You know how the pride of others hurts me, and so I place my hurt into your hands also. Pray for me, that I would grow each day in magnanimity, mercy, and love.

Our Lady, Undoer of Knots, please give me the desire to truly forgive and the humility to ask for forgiveness. Free me from my stubborn ways, and let me be free from the stubbornness of others. Envy and pride have caused this knot; now please undo it so that we can live in charity, peace, and freedom.

Please pray for me, and for those who join me in these knots. I also want to unite my prayers with those of Pope Francis, asking that lasting peace may be granted to the Holy Land. Amen.

Pray the Rosary, offering it in petition for those who betrayed you, and others who have been betrayed. Pray also for peace in the Holy Land.

Stepping Out in Faith

Take some time to think about the questions below. Then answer them as honestly as you can so that your heart can continue to grow more and more peaceful.

- Who do you envy? Why?
- Are you aware that someone is envious of you? Who? Of what are they envious?
- What can you do to discourage it?
- Are you prideful? In what way?
- Are there things that spark your pridefulness? How might you avoid them?
- Have you been affected by the pride of someone else? How?

Make a concrete resolution to take one step toward peace in your heart today.

Day Nine: The Cenacle

The Knot of Affliction

I have a dogmatic certainty: God is in every person's life. God is in everyone's life. Even if the life of a person has been a disaster, even if it is destroyed by vices, drugs or anything else—God is in this person's life. You can, you must try to seek God in every human life. Although the life of a person is a land full of thorns and weeds, there is always a space in which the good seed can grow. You have to trust God.

—Pope Francis[1]

We all face afflictions of one kind or another. Some of us suffer from many kinds of affliction at once. Affliction is a state of misery that can be the result of illness, adversity, misfortune, infirmity, hardship, disease, or persecution. While there can be afflictions that come and go, affliction generally is a long-term condition.

Affliction is hard to bear because it reminds us that we are weak and dependent. It makes us feel helpless. It can wear us down to the point that we almost don't want to care anymore. This is especially true when we suffer from an affliction that has no apparent cause or cure. Sometimes, affliction requires us to accept assistance from others and most of us hate doing that. We want to be independent, capable, and able to handle things on our own.

There's a tendency for people to scorn those who are afflicted. Some of that is the result of prejudice, and some of it is because the afflicted remind us of our own human frailty. We don't want to think that we could be like them, because it's disturbing to picture ourselves suffering as they are. This is part of what makes Blessed Mother Teresa of Calcutta a saint. The afflicted didn't scare her—in fact, she loved them as she loved the Lord himself. She and her Missionaries of Charity serve them out of love for Christ.

The knot of affliction can become all-consuming. Affliction itself is a knot, and it can cause other, related knots along with it. For example, the affliction of being disabled after a car accident would be the main knot, so to speak. But the fact that we're disabled creates other knots—absence from work, loss of income, financial distress, depression, and perhaps changes in relationships—that compound the knot of affliction.

Affliction isn't something new; it's been around since the days of the Psalmist:

> Be gracious to me, LORD, for I am in distress;
> affliction is wearing down my eyes,
> my throat and my insides.
> My life is worn out by sorrow,
> and my years by sighing.
> My strength fails in my affliction;
> my bones are wearing down. (Ps 31:10–11)

Affliction can really wear us down unless, of course, we seek help from Our Lady, Undoer of Knots, to undo our knot of affliction.

Signs from the Holy Land: In the Upper Room

Pope Francis, accompanied by the Ordinaries of the Holy Land, celebrated Mass in the Cenacle when he visited. This in itself was remarkable, because it's located in Jerusalem on Israeli property and the Israeli authorities don't usually allow the Eucharist to be celebrated there. However, they made an exception for the Holy Father.

The Cenacle, or Upper Room, is a second-story room that commemorates the place in which Jesus and his apostles shared the Last Supper, and also where he appeared to them after his Resurrection and the Holy Spirit descended upon Mary and Jesus' followers on Pentecost. It's not the actual room—this one was built in the twelfth century—but it gives visitors a good idea of what these events might have been like.[2]

Before beginning his homily, Pope Francis expressed his gratitude for the presence of the clerics from the Eastern Orthodox Church—yet another symbol of his efforts to reach out to the "other lung" of the Church and a sign of his yearning for peace in the Holy Land. The words of his homily, I think, are strikingly significant for all those who suffer from affliction. There are six points in particular that I'd like to touch upon.

First, the pope explained, *by helping the afflicted—and accepting help from others when afflicted—we imitate Christ,* who washed the feet of the apostles at the Last Supper.

> The Upper Room speaks to us of service, of Jesus giving the disciples an example by washing their feet. Washing one another's feet signifies welcoming, accepting, loving and serving one another. It means serving the poor, the sick and the outcast.[3]

Second, in the Upper Room *through the celebration of the Eucharist, the Lord taught us that affliction speaks of sacrifice*. In the words of Pope Francis:

> In every eucharistic celebration Jesus offers himself for us to the Father, so that we too can be united with him, offering to God our lives, our work, our joys and our sorrows . . . offering everything as a spiritual sacrifice.[4]

Third, the Upper Room *speaks not only of sacrifice, but of friendship and community.* When we are afflicted, we really need the love and support of our family and friends.

> Even if they are helpless to stop our suffering, they can ease the burden with their prayerful presence: "No longer do I call you servants— Jesus said to the Twelve—but I have called you friends" (Jn 15:15). The Lord makes us his friends, he reveals God's will to us and he gives us his very self. This is the most beautiful part of being a Christian and, especially, of being a priest: becoming a friend of the Lord Jesus.[5]

More than anything, the Upper Room reminds us that God does not abandon us in our affliction, no matter how we feel in the moment.

> The Upper Room reminds us of the Teacher's farewell and his promise to return to his friends: "When I go . . . I will come again and will take you to myself, that where I am you may be also" (Jn 14:3). Jesus does not leave us, nor does he ever

> abandon us; he precedes us to the house of the Father, where he desires to bring us as well.[6]

If we look to the Upper Room, we can find our source of strength and courage in and during affliction.

> The Upper Room reminds us of sharing, fraternity, harmony and peace among ourselves. How much love and goodness has flowed from the Upper Room! How much charity has gone forth from here, like a river from its source, beginning as a stream and then expanding and becoming a great torrent. All the saints drew from this source; and hence the great river of the Church's holiness continues to flow: from the Heart of Christ, from the Eucharist and from the Holy Spirit.[7]

Finally, Pope Francis assures us, the Upper Room reminds us that we are part of a family who loves and cares for us, even in our affliction.

> The Upper Room reminds us of the birth of the new family, the Church, established by the risen Jesus; a family that has a Mother, the Virgin Mary. Christian families belong to this great family, and in it they find the light and strength to press on and be renewed, amid the challenges and difficulties of life. All God's children, of every people and language, are invited and called to be part of this

> great family, as brothers and sisters and sons and daughters of the one Father in heaven.[8]

On the day my group visited the Upper Room, I was painfully disappointed to discover that the room itself was closed to the public because Pope Francis would be celebrating Mass there later that same day. Of all the Holy Land sites, that was one that I absolutely did not want to miss! With all my heart, I wanted to stand in the room where Jesus had the Last Supper with his apostles, witnessing the institution of the holy Eucharist and the Catholic priesthood. I wanted to imagine what it was like to hear the sound of the wind and see the tongues of fire above the heads of Mary and the 120 other men and women at the first Pentecost. I wanted to breathe in the presence of the Holy Spirit while praying the *Veni Sancte Spiritus*. Unfortunately, I had to be content with seeing and imagining everything from outside, in the courtyard.

As an experienced journalist, I knew that, when things don't work out as planned, I just had to shift gears and make the best of it. So, I decided to take in what I could from the building's exterior. I stood in the courtyard and looked up at the narrow windows above me. I strained to "hear" what was going on inside, but instead I began to "hear" what was happening out on the streets—the merchants in the markets, mothers calling, children laughing, and the townspeople gossiping about Jesus the Nazarene, who claimed he could rise from the dead.

I could "see" Roman soldiers shuffling along, sneering about how they'd gotten rid of that trouble-maker, Jesus. Then it occurred to me that, although the Holy Spirit descended upon the disciples inside the Upper Room, the Church itself sprang to life outside of it—on the streets, where Peter and the other disciples, filled with the Spirit, praised God, began proclaiming the Good News, and converted thousands in a single day.

The Church had been conceived in the Upper Room, but it was born on the streets of Jerusalem.

I looked around the city of Jerusalem and imagined the apostles making their way along the steep inclines and narrow stone streets, preaching about Christ crucified and risen and inviting all to the baptism and salvation.

I wondered whether the disciples had stood on the same spot I was standing as they glorified God and related their amazement over what had transpired in the Upper Room. Did they talk about what they would do next? I wanted to think so.

I looked at the windows again. This time, I didn't feel disappointment but rather great gratitude and joy. I was in the birthplace of the Church—the place from where the apostles traveled to the ends of the world to lead others to Christ. They went forth in the Spirit of love, and because of that, I was able to stand below the Cenacle windows and give thanks to God for what had happened there.

Viewing Our Interior Landscape

Affliction can leave us feeling stressed and distressed, not knowing which way to turn or where to go next. Physical affliction can make us feel weak and forlorn. Emotional affliction can make us feel depleted and distraught. Spiritual affliction can make us bitter and resentful. And yet, all affliction is an opportunity to persevere in faith.

Are you suffering from a chronic disease or even a terminal illness? The ups and downs of maintaining health can put wear and tear on both body and mind. Do you struggle with an emotional or mental affliction? You, too, need the Holy Father's words in the Cenacle to become reality, and to experience service, friendship, and love.

Maybe your affliction is situational, like scandal or an abusive relationship. Are you tormented by horrible memories or unrelenting guilt? Have you suffered financial collapse? Have your children or someone else close to you left the Church? Are you helplessly standing by as someone you love endures affliction? All of these kinds of affliction can be frustrating and heart-wrenching, especially when there's no apparent solution.

The Blessed Mother suffered unspeakable affliction as she accompanied Jesus through his passion and crucifixion. She was so intimately united with her son that she felt his pain and sensed his torment. She unites herself with us, too, because we are her children and she feels our affliction profoundly.

We need only place our hearts and these knots of affliction into her hands. As she waited with the disciples in the Upper Room for the coming of the Spirit, she'll wait with you until the Spirit comes to lift you out of your misery.

The Journey Begins: Let Us Pray for Patience

Our Lady, Undoer of Knots,

I'm being crushed by this affliction. I don't understand why God allows it, nor do I understand how to cope with it. All I know is that you somehow understand all of this, because you're so close to God and to me.

Sometimes not knowing the how or why is as difficult to bear as the affliction itself. Please help me to accept my inability to understand, and give me the strength and courage to endure this knot of affliction that burdens me [name the affliction]. You know all the people affected by this affliction—please also give them the strength and courage that they need.

Mother, take this knot from me, and work through it in your loving, capable way. Teach me how to persist patiently, as you did while watching our Lord suffer his passion and crucifixion.

Help me to remember the message of the Cenacle—that Jesus will send the Spirit to encourage and enlighten me.

As you work on this knot of affliction, please work on my heart so that I can truly trust in Jesus' promise that he will come again and take me to himself. Please pray for me, and for those who join me in these knots. I also want to unite my prayers with those of Pope Francis, asking that lasting peace may be granted to the Holy Land. Amen.

Pray the Rosary, offering it in petition for the alleviation of this affliction and others who suffer this affliction. Pray also for peace in the Holy Land.

Stepping Out in Faith

Take some time to think about the questions below. Then answer them as honestly as you can so that your heart can continue to grow more and more peaceful.

- What is your affliction? What makes this affliction so hard for you to bear? Why?
- Do you know others who suffer similar affliction? Who?
- What can you learn from them?

- What can you offer them?
- What has this affliction taught you about yourself?

Make a concrete resolution to take one step toward peace in your heart today.

Conclusion

My trip to the Holy Land caught me off guard in many ways. At first, I was shocked at having been chosen to go. I knew other journalists that I highly respected had applied; I assumed they'd get to go rather than me. But, miraculously, God chose me and I'm humbled and grateful. It was a life-changing experience.

Being in the Holy Land has given both my writing and prayer life greater depth. I use a lot of scripture passages in my work, and they all came alive for me as we made our way along the Sea of Galilee, to the Mount of the Beatitudes and Masada, Qumran (where the Dead Sea Scrolls were discovered), to Nazareth and Bethlehem, and down to Jerusalem. Jesus, Peter, John, Mary, Joseph, Herod, Abraham, and David—they were all walking along beside me. They became so real for me that I could have almost reached out and touched them. Saying the Rosary and attending Mass are completely different for me now. I "see" and "feel" each mystery as I pray them. At Mass, I "remember" the places and scenes mentioned because I was there. It's a remarkable privilege that is difficult to describe.

My second shock came through Our Lady, Undoer of Knots. The knots that I had expected her to begin working on while I was there were not the ones she ended up undoing. I fully expected to have a number of work-related tangles resolved, like how to better hone my skills, who I should (or shouldn't) write for, and what my next project should be. I wanted obstacles removed and directions given.

Some of that did happen, but only an extremely small amount when compared to the knots she tackled in my personal life. Around every corner (really), I encountered a symbol, situation, or conversation that directly correlated with some hardship or puzzlement my family and I had been facing. For some, I received specific answers; for others, I was given guidance; and for still others, the assurance that all would be well. Most certainly I was carrying my family in my heart throughout the trip, but I hadn't anticipated that in such a unique way they'd become the underlying reason for it.

Most of those knots are too private to share with you, but there is one that I can. In Bethlehem, just around the corner from the Church of the Nativity, lies the Cave of the Shepherds, carved into the side of the hill. This is the place where the angels appeared to the shepherds on Christmas Eve and proclaimed the Good News of peace on earth, goodwill to men. There was something about the cave that really gripped me, and I just didn't want to leave. But, our time was up, and we had to move on. I snapped my last picture, muttered a final prayer, and turned to hurry out of the cave. Just to the left of the doorway, I saw her: an image of the Mother Thrice Admirable, Queen and Victress of Schoenstatt enthroned in the cave wall. It was obvious that she hadn't been left there by other pilgrims—she was there permanently, with the picture frame embedded in the rock!

I couldn't believe it! I shook from head to toe and sobbed. It's our Schoenstatt custom to have a prayer corner (which we call a home shrine) in our homes in which we enthrone the Mother Thrice Admirable. Each family member chooses a symbol from the home shrine that represents them—the candle, crucifix, tabernacle, altar, and so on. This is a way of uniting the family with each other and with the universal Church, as the symbols are the same ones you'd find in any Catholic church and in the Schoenstatt Marian shrines around the world. In our family home shrine, our middle son chose to "be" the Mother Thrice Admirable picture. He'd been especially on my heart that day, with some pretty tough knots, and seeing "him" in the cave gave me assurance that Our Lady, Undoer of Knots, already was at work on those knots.

This is how it will be for you, too. Our Lady, Undoer of Knots, will untangle even the most vicious knots in your life—if only you entrust them to her. One day, you'll be surprised like I was in the Cave of the Shepherds in Bethlehem. It might not be as dramatic as my experience, but somehow you'll know that the knot has begun to unsnarl in Our Lady's hands.

I think about my days in the Holy Land with unbounded gratitude and ardent yearning to return. The places I visited, experiences I shared, and knots untied will forever rest in my heart. If you've never been to the Holy Land, I hope this book gives you an idea of what it's like and instills in you the yearning to go there; I hope that it urges you to pilgrimage there soon. If you have been to the Holy Land, I hope this book brings back wonderful memories, brings you even closer to our Lord, and imbues in you a deepening confidence in his love for you.

More than anything, I hope that *Our Lady, Undoer of Knots: A Living Novena* leads you on a spiritual journey that will deepen your faith, increase your love for our Blessed Mother, and commence the undoing of the knots in your life. *Our Lady, Undoer of Knots, pray for us!*

Appendix 1:
On the Origin of Our Lady, Undoer of Knots

Although it has only recently become popular, the image of Our Lady, Undoer of Knots, dates back to the seventeenth century. A German nobleman, Wolfgang Langenmantel (1586–1637) was having difficulty in his marriage of some years to his wife, Sophie. In 1612, the marriage began teetering on the brink of collapse, and the couple was considering divorce. In an act of desperation to save his marriage, Wolfgang visited Jesuit Fr. Jakob Rem (1546–1618), who lived in a monastery at the University of Ingolstadt, about seventy kilometers north of Augsburg.

Wolfgang visited Fr. Rem four times over the course of twenty-eight days, each time receiving advice from this priest who was honored for his holiness, wisdom, and exceptional intelligence. Whenever they met, Wolfgang and Fr. Rem prayed together and venerated the Blessed Mother. Early on September 28, 1615—the day of their last visit together—Fr. Rem had spent time in the monastery chapel praying before an image of Mary titled *Our Lady of the Snows*. In Germany at that time, it was customary for the bride and groom to have their hands gently bound with a silk ribbon during the wedding ceremony—a symbol of the unbreakable bond between spouses. When they met later that day, Wolfgang gave his marriage ribbon to Fr. Rem. Upon receiving the ribbon, Fr. Rem solemnly lifted it up and gestured, as though untying the knots that had occurred over the years. The ribbon miraculously became intensely white. Through this miracle, Wolfgang and Sophie were reunited and continued their marriage.

Many years later, Wolfgang's grandson, Hieronymus Ambrosius Langenmantel (1641–1718), a priest and canon lawyer, donated a family altar to the Church of St. Peter am Perlach in Augsburg. The altar was to commemorate the turn of the century in the year 1700. Fr. Hieronymus wanted the altar to represent the history of the Langenmantel family, and so he had the altarpiece dedicated to "the Blessed Virgin of Good Counsel."

In addition, painter Johann Melchior Georg Schmittdner was commissioned to create a painting for the Langenmantel family altar. Basing his painting on the story of Wolfgang, Sophie, and Fr. Rem, Schmittdner decided to depict Mary untying the knots of the ribbon of married life. He included the crushing of the serpent to highlight Mary as the Immaculate Conception who, by virtue of her exemption from stain of original sin, valiantly opposes the devil. The dove represents Mary as the Bride of the Holy Spirit.

Angels assist the Blessed Mother: one presents the knots of our lives to her, while another angel presents the ribbon, freed from knots, to us. Underneath Mary, the worried noble Wolfgang, accompanied by the Archangel Raphael, walks toward a monastery.

Although the Langenmantel family's story receded over the years, the image of Mary as Undoer of Knots continued to become better known. The painting has survived wars, revolutions, and secular opposition, and continues to this day to be venerated by thousands of pilgrims each year in the Church of St. Peter am Perlach in Augsburg.

It's notable that there's a link between the devotions of the Apostolic Movement of Schoenstatt, founded by Fr. Joseph Kentenich and mentioned earlier in this book, and the devotion to Our Lady, Undoer of Knots. Both devotions have one person in common: Fr. Jakob Rem.

During his time at the University of Ingolstadt, Fr. Rem worked with a Marian Sodality, the mission of which was to generate a great Catholic renewal. In 1604, as the sodalists were singing the "Litany of Loretto," Fr. Rem had an illumination that Mary's favorite title was "Mother Most Admirable." An ensuing vision prompted him to instruct the choir to repeat that invocation three times, and this became the title under which the students venerated Mary, *Mother Thrice Admirable of Ingolstadt.*[1]

In 1912, a parallel story took place in Schoenstatt, Germany. Fr. Kentenich was assigned as spiritual director of the students of the Pallotine Seminary in Vallendar

(Schoenstatt), Germany. Under Fr. Kentenich's guidance, the young men were inspired to form a Marian Sodality, with the desire to be the instruments of a great Catholic renewal. Fr. Kentenich discovered Fr. Rem's story in a book and shared it with the sodalists, who immediately felt that it perfectly captured their spirit and longing. They chose *Mother Thrice Admirable* as the title for their own image of Mary, replacing Ingolstadt with Schoenstatt. Today, throughout the world, Mary is venerated in the Schoenstatt Movement as *Mother Thrice Admirable, Queen and Victress of Schoenstatt.*

Appendix 2: How to Pray the Rosary

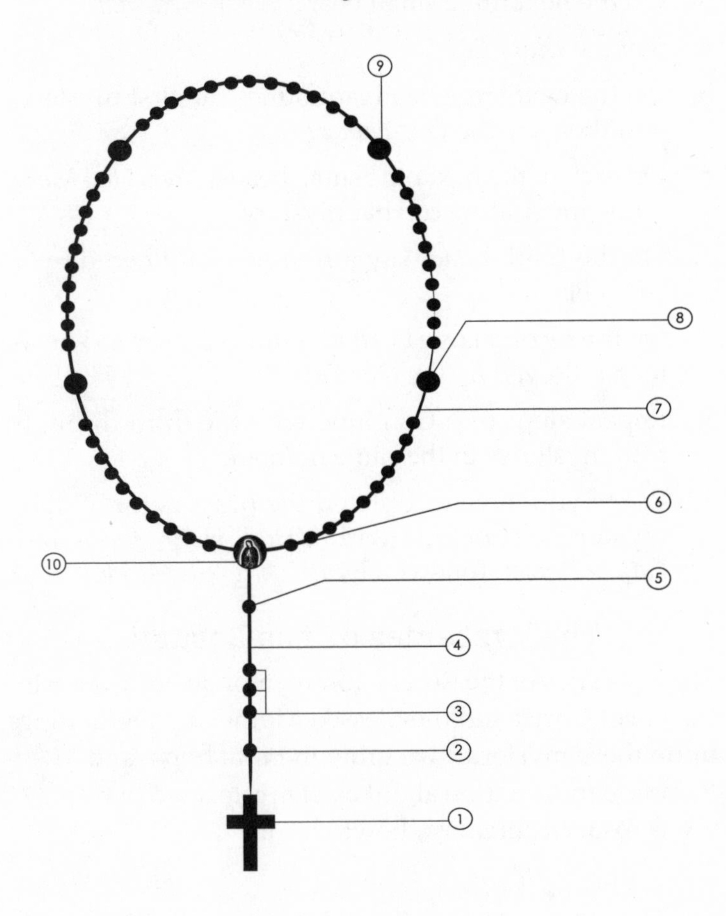

1. Make the Sign of the Cross and say the *Apostles' Creed*.
2. On the first large bead, say the *Our Father*.
3. On the next three small beads, say a *Hail Mary*.
4. Say the *Glory Be*.
5. On the next large bead, announce the first mystery, and then say the *Our Father*.
6. On each of the next nine small beads, say a *Hail Mary* while meditating on that mystery.
7. On the tenth bead, say a *Hail Mary* followed by a *Glory Be*.
8. On the second large bead announce the second mystery, followed by the *Our Father*.
9. Repeat steps 6–7. Continue with the third through fifth mysteries in the same manner.
10. When you have completed the prayers for all five mysteries, conclude with a *Hail, Holy Queen* and *Fatima Prayer*, followed by *Prayer to St. Michael*.

The Mysteries of the Rosary

The mysteries of the Rosary commemorate key events in the life of Christ and the Blessed Mother. By meditating upon these mysteries we grow in faith, hope, and love. For more information about each mystery, go to http://www.rosary-center.org/howto.html.

- *The Joyful Mysteries* (Monday, Saturday): The Annunciation, the Visitation, the Nativity, the Presentation, the Finding of Jesus in the Temple
- *The Sorrowful Mysteries* (Tuesday, Friday): The Agony in the Garden, the Scourging at the Pillar, the Crowning with Thorns, the Carrying of the Cross, the Crucifixion
- *The Luminous Mysteries* (Thursday): The Baptism of the Lord, the Wedding of Cana, the Proclamation of the Kingdom, the Transfiguration, the Institution of the Eucharist
- *The Glorious Mysteries* (Wednesday, Sunday): The Resurrection, the Ascension, the Descent of the Holy Spirit, the Assumption, the Coronation of Mary as Queen of Heaven

The Prayers of the Rosary

Apostles' Creed

I believe in God, the Father Almighty, Creator of heaven and earth; and in Jesus Christ, His only Son, our Lord; Who was conceived by the Holy Spirit, born of the Virgin Mary, suffered under Pontius Pilate, was crucified, died, and was buried. He descended into hell; the third day he arose again from the dead. He ascended into heaven, and sits at the right hand of God, the Father Almighty; from thence he shall come to judge the living and the dead. *I believe in the Holy Spirit, the Holy Catholic Church, the communion of saints, the forgiveness of sins, the resurrection of the body and life everlasting. Amen.*

Our Father

Our Father, who art in heaven, hallowed be Thy name; Thy kingdom come; Thy will be done on earth as it is in heaven. *Give us this day our daily bread; and forgive us our trespasses as we forgive those who trespass against us; and lead us not into temptation; but deliver us from evil. Amen.*

Hail Mary

Hail Mary, full of grace, the Lord is with thee; blessed art thou among women, and blessed is the fruit of thy womb, Jesus. *Holy Mary, Mother of God, pray for us sinners, now and at the hour of our death. Amen.*

Glory Be

Glory be to the Father, and to the Son, and to the Holy Spirit. *As it was in the beginning, is now, and ever shall be, world without end. Amen.*

Hail, Holy Queen

Hail, Holy Queen, Mother of Mercy, our life, our sweetness and our hope! To thee do we cry, poor banished children of Eve; to thee do we send up our sighs, mourning and weeping in this vale of tears. Turn then, most gracious advocate, thine eyes of mercy toward us, and after this our exile, show unto us the blessed fruit of thy womb, Jesus. O clement, O loving, O sweet Virgin Mary!

V. Pray for us, O Holy Mother of God.

R. That we may be made worthy of the promises of Christ.

Let us pray. O GOD, whose only begotten Son, by his life, death, and resurrection, has purchased for us the rewards of eternal life, grant, we beseech Thee, that meditating upon these mysteries of the Most Holy Rosary of the Blessed Virgin Mary, we may imitate what they contain and obtain what they promise, through the same Christ Our Lord. Amen.

Fatima Prayer

O my Jesus, forgive us our sins, save us from the fires of hell, lead all souls to heaven, especially those who have most need of your mercy.

Prayer to St. Michael

Saint Michael the Archangel, defend us in battle.
Be our protection against the wickedness and snares of the devil.
May God rebuke him, we humbly pray.
And do Thou, O Prince of the Heavenly Host—
by the Divine Power of God—cast into hell, Satan and all the evil spirits, who roam throughout the world seeking the ruin of souls. Amen.

Notes

Introduction

1. "Address of the Holy Father Francis, Prayer for the Marian Day on the Occasion of the Year of Faith," *The Holy See*, October 12, 2013, accessed March 3, 2015, http://w2.vatican.va/content/francesco/en/speeches/2013/october/documents/papa-francesco_20131012_preghiera-mariana.html, accessed March 3, 2015.

2. Rocco Palmo, "The Great 'Untier' – For Francis, There's Something About Mary," *Whispers in the Loggia* (blog), Sunday, October 13, accessed March 21, 2015, http://whispersintheloggia.blogspot.com/2013/10/the-great-untier-for-francis-theres.html.

Day One: The Knot of Injustice

1. "Message of Pope Francis for World Youth Day 2014," *Salt and Light Media*: WYD Central, February 6, 2014, accessed March 21, 2015, http://wydcentral.org/message-of-pope-francis-for-the-29th-world-youth-day-2014/.

2. "Pope Francis' homily during Mass at International Stadium in Amman," *Salt and Light Media* (blog), May 24, 2014, accessed March 22, 2015, http://saltandlighttv.org/blog/apostolic/pope-francis-homily-during-mass-at-international-stadium-in-amman.

3. Ibid.

Day Two: The Knot of Separation

1. "Pope Francis: Divisions among Christians wound Christ," *Rome Reports*, October 8, 2014, accessed March 22, 2015, http://www.romereports.com/pg158633-pope-francis-divisions-among-christians-wound-christ-en.

2. "The Promising Journey: 'Peace Will Bring Countless Benefits,'" *The Holy Land Review* 7, no. 3 (Summer 2014): 28.

3. "Pope Pleas for Courage for Peace Process During Bethlehem Visit," *Edizioni Terra Santa*, May 25, 2014, accessed March 22, 2015, http://www.terrasanta.net/tsx/articolo.jsp?wi_number=6523&wi_codseq=HL010%20&language=en.

4. "The Promising Journey: 'Peace Will Bring Countless Benefits,'" *The Holy Land Review* 7, no. 3 (Summer 2014): 28.

Day Three: The Knot of Confusion

1. "Pope Francis: Trust in the Lord, Not in Yourself," *Vatican Radio*, March 20, 2014, accessed March 22, 2015, http://en.radiovaticana.va/storico/2014/03/20/pope_francis_trust_in_the_lord%2C_not_in_yourself/en1-783118.

2. "Pope in Palestine: May Israelis and Palestinians Find the 'Courage of Peace' to Create 'Two States,'" *AsiaNews*, May 25, 2014, accessed March 22, 2015, http://www.asianews.it/news-en/Pope-in-Palestine:-May-Israelis-and-Palestinians-find-the-courage-of-peace-to-create-two-states-31170.html.

Day Four: The Knot of Hopelessness

1. "The Law of Love: Pope Francis," *EWTN* as taken from *L'Osservatore Romano* Weekly Edition in English from June 19, 2013, accessed March 22, 2015, http://www.ewtn.com/library/PAPALDOC/f1genaud12.htm.

2. "Pope Francis: Discourse to Priests, Religious, and Seminarians in Holy Land," *Vatican Radio*, May 26, 2014, accessed March 22, 2015, http://en.radiovaticana.va/news/2014/05/26/pope_francis_to_priests,_religious,_seminarians_in_holy_land/1101033.

3. "Massada (Masada), Israel," *Israel Ministry of Tourism*, accessed April 8, 2015, http://www.goisrael.com/Tourism_Eng/Articles/Attractions/Pages/Massada.aspx.

Day Five: The Knots of Grief and Loss

1. Lumen Fidei, 16. "Message of Pope Francis for the 29th World Youth Day 2014", *Salt and Light Media*: WYD Central (blog), February 6, 2014, accessed March 22, 2015, http://wydcentral.org/message-of-pope-francis-for-the-29th-world-youth-day-2014/.

2. "Pilgrimage to the Holy Land, Address of Paul VI to the Armenian Patriarch Yegheshe Derderian," *The Holy See*, January 4, 1964, accessed January 4, 2015, http://www.vatican.va/holy_father/paul_vi/speeches/1964/documents/hf_p-vi_spe_19640104_derderian_en.html.

3. Francis X. Rocca, "Pope Francis and the Patriarch," *The Holy Land Review* 7, no. 3 (Summer 2014): 38–39.

4. "Address of Pope Francis, Ecumenical Celebration on the Occasion of the 50th Anniversary of the Meeting

Between Pope Paul VI and Patriarch Athenagoras in Jerusalem," *The Holy See*, May 25, 2014, accessed March 22, 2015, http://w2.vatican.va/content/francesco/en/speeches/2014/may/documents/papa-francesco_20140525_terra-santa-celebrazione-ecumenica.pdf.

Day Six: The Knot of Discord

1. "Address of Pope Francis to Bishops of the Episcopal Conference of Guinea on the 'Ad Limina' Visit," *The Holy See*, March 24, 2015, accessed March 23, 2015, http://w2.vatican.va/content/francesco/en/speeches/2014/march/documents/papa-francesco_20140324_ad-limina-guinea.pdf.

2. "Reaching out to Muslims & Jews: 'Work for peace and justice,'" *The Holy Land Review* 7, no. 3 (Summer 2014): 34.

3. "Western Wall Facts and Figures: The Stones of the Western Wall," *Western Wall Heritage Foundation*, accessed February 14, 2015, http://english.thekotel.org/content.asp?id=28.

Day Seven: The Knot of Betrayal

1. Kerri Lenartowick, "Pope: A Christian refusing to serve others is a 'pagan,'" *Catholic News Agency*, December 18, 2013, accessed March 23, 2015, http://www.catholicnewsagency.com/news/pope-a-christian-refusing-to-serve-others-is-a-pagan/, accessed March 23, 2015.

2. "Pope Francis at Yad Vashem," *YadVashem.org*, May 26, 2014, accessed March 23, 2015, http://www.yadvashem.org/yv/en/about/events/pope/francis/speech.asp.

3. Matthew E. Bunson, "Catholic Martyrs of the Holocaust," *Catholic Answers*, accessed January 4, 2015, http://www.catholic.com/magazine/articles/catholic-martyrs-of-the-holocaust.

4. Ibid.

Day Eight: The Knots of Envy and Pride

1. "Full Text: Pope Francis' Wednesday General audience Address," *The Catholic World Report* (blog), June 12, 2013, accessed March 23, 2015, http://www.catholicworldreport.com/Blog/2320/full_text_pope_francis_wednesday_general_audience_address.aspx.

2. St. John Chrysostom, Hom. in 2 Cor. 27,3–4:PG 61,588.

3. Daniel C. Eisenbud, "Francis Beseeches Grand Mufti to Disavow Temple Mount Strife," *Jerusalem Post*, May 27, 2014, accessed April 6, 2015, http://www.jpost.com/Middle-East/Francis-beseeches-Grand-Mufti-to-disavow-Temple-Mount-strife-354444.

4. "Pope Francis Visits the Grand Mufti and the Western Wall," *Salt and Light Media* (blog), May 26, 2014, accessed March 23, 2015, http://saltandlighttv.org/blog/apostolic/pope-francis-address-at-the-visit-of-the-grand-mufti-of-jerusalem.

5. Ibid.

6. "Experience Jerusalem," *Austrian Hospice of the Holy Family*, accessed February 14, 2015, http://www.austrianhospice.com/experience-jerusalem.htm.

Day Nine: The Knot of Afflicition

1. Antonio Spadaro, S.J, "Big Heart Open to God," *America: The National Catholic Review*, September, 30, 2013, accessed March 23, 2015, http: / / americamagazine.org / pope-interview.

2. "Last Supper Room, Jerusalem," *Sacred Destinations*, accessed April 6, 2015, http: / / www.sacred-destinations.com / israel / jerusalem-last-supper-room.

3. "Pope Francis: Homily in the Upper Room," *Vatican Radio*, May 26, 2014, accessed March 23, 2015, http: / / en.radiovaticana.va / news / 2014 / 05 / 26 / pope_francis_homily_in_the_upper_room / 1101035.

4. Ibid.

5. Ibid.

6. Ibid.

7. Ibid.

8. Ibid.

Appendix 1

1. Fr. Jonathan Niehaus, *200 Questions about Schoenstatt* (Waukesha, WI: Schoenstatt Fathers, 2002), #13.

Marge Fenelon is a Catholic author, blogger, speaker, and longtime contributor to a variety of Catholic and secular publications and websites, including *Our Sunday Visitor*, *National Catholic Register*, and *Catholic News Service*. Her column, *The Whirl*, appears in the *Milwaukee Catholic Herald*, and her blog, *Catholic to the Core*, is on *Patheos*. Fenelon is the author of a number of books related to Marian devotion and Catholic family life, including *Imitating Mary*.

Fenelon is a regular guest on Catholic radio, including *Relevant Radio's Morning Air* and EWTN's *Son Rise Morning Show*. She earned a bachelor's degree in mass communications from the University of Wisconsin-Milwaukee and a certificate in spiritual mentoring from Cardinal Stritch University. Fenelon also holds a certificate in Marian studies from the International Marian Research Institute and is a member of the Mariological Society of America. Fenelon is a consecrated member of the Apostolic Movement of Schoenstatt and an instructor for the Archdiocese of Milwaukee's Permanent Deacon Wives Program. She completed an intensive training program for foreign journalists by the Pontifical University of Holy Cross in conjunction with the Vatican Office of Communications in Rome in 2014. Fenelon and her husband, Mark, have four grown children and live in Milwaukee.

Founded in 1865, Ave Maria Press, a ministry of the Congregation of Holy Cross, is a Catholic publishing company that serves the spiritual and formative needs of the Church and its schools, institutions, and ministers; Christian individuals and families; and others seeking spiritual nourishment.

For a complete listing of titles from

Ave Maria Press

Sorin Books

Forest of Peace

Christian Classics

visit www.avemariapress.com

AVE | Ave Maria Press
Notre Dame, IN
A Ministry of the United States Province of Holy Cross